A Fragile Stone

THE
EMOTIONAL LIFE
OF
SIMON PETER

MICHAEL CARD

IVP Books
An imprint of InterVarsity Press
Downers Grove, Illinois

InterVarsity Press
P.O. Box 1400, Downers Grove, IL 60515-1426
World Wide Web: www.ivpress.com
E-mail: email@ivpress.com

InterVarsity Press® is the book-publishing division of InterVarsity Christian Fellowship/USA®, a student movement active on campus at hundreds of universities, colleges and schools of nursing in the United States of America,
and a member movement of the International Fellowship of Evangelical Students. For information about local and
regional activities, write Public Relations Dept., InterVarsity Christian Fellowship/USA, 6400 Schroeder Rd.,
P.O. Box 7895, Madison, WI 53707-7895, or visit the IVCF website at <www.intervarsity.org>.

Unless otherwise indicated, all Scripture quotations are taken from the Holy Bible, New Living Translation,
copyright ©1996. Used by permission of Tyndale House Publishers, Inc., Wheaton, Illinois 60189. All rights
reserved.

Design: Cindy Kiple
Images: Jim Linna/Getty Images

USA ISBN-10: 0-8308-3445-1
    ISBN-13: 978-0-8308-3445-7

Printed in the United States of America ∞

Library of Congress Cataloging-in-Publication Data
Card, Michael, 1957-
    A fragile stone: the emotional life of Simon Peter / Michael Card.
    p. cm.
Includes bibliographical references.
    ISBN 0-8308-2372-7 (alk. paper)
    1. Peter, the Apostle, Saint. 2. Apostles—Biography. I. Title.
BS2515.C37 2003
225.9'2—dc21
                                                    2003006826

P   17 16 15 14 13 12 11 10 9 8 7 6 5 4 3 2 1
Y   18 17 16 15 14 13 12 11 10 09 08 07 06

If we are to recognize and understand qualities like

humility and servanthood in biblical characters like Peter,

God knows we need to have before us living examples.

This book is dedicated to

C. Michael Smith,

who constantly came to mind as an exemplar

as I sought to understand what Peter must have been like.

He possesses a true pastor's heart

(by no virtue of his own, he would insist).

Mike, if I had not known you,

I could have never appreciated what the Scriptures

reveal about Simon Peter the missionary pastor.

Contents

Foreword

A *Fragile Stone*—a fitting title indeed. Peter, the most well-developed character in the Gospels aside from Jesus, is presented in all his misery and magnificence. Just as Paul is remembered as the one who persecuted the church before his own conversion on the road to Damascus, Peter is remembered forever as the apostle who denied Christ. The Rock on whom Jesus would build his church proved to be a sand pile. When he attempted to walk on water, the Rock sank like a stone.

Peter rebuked Jesus when the Lord spoke of his impending death in Jerusalem, and Jesus called him "Satan." His various boasts about his unbending loyalty to Jesus proved hollow in the courtyard of the high priest Caiaphas. When Paul confronted Peter for his inconsistency and hypocrisy in drawing back from table fellowship with Gentile Christians in Antioch, under pressure from some Jewish Christians who arrived later in Jerusalem, Paul got in Peter's face "because he was clearly out of line" (Galatians 2:11). Even after the anointing of the Holy Spirit at Pentecost, the undisputed leader of the apostolic community was yet a people-pleaser!

Michael Card does not mince words. In spite of all the powerful evidence to the contrary, Peter was the "closest friend" Jesus ever had.

What comfort Peter offers to the bruised, bent and broken! He enters the heroic Hebrew pantheon of Abraham, our father in faith and the great old man of the First Testament, who unscrupulously palmed off his wife, Sarah, as his sister and allowed Pharaoh to bed her in order to save his own skin; Isaac, who did something similar with Rebekah; Jacob, who stole his brother's birthright; and beloved King David, an adulterer and murderer, a simple, ambitious and violent man whom Yahweh denied the privilege of building the temple because he had shed so much blood (1 Chronicles 22:8). Peter was a weak, flawed, sinful man who, nonetheless, is defined by what the love of Jesus Christ wrought in him.

Perhaps what separates Peter from many of us is that he honestly admitted his sins and failures. He never warped his conscience by rationalization, denial, lying or allowing his heart to harden in the face of truth. Conversely, when we refuse to face our own truth and minimize, justify and rationalize our sin, we have effectively parted company with Jesus Christ. Peter's radical honesty and searing contrition (he wept bitterly) encourage us to courageously confront the truth of our own brokenness. God easily and eagerly forgives our weaknesses; only when we pretend to be sinners and pretend to be forgiven does the spiritual life become a charade of pseudo-repentance and pseudo-bliss.

The author's unabashed love for Peter shines through these pages and permits him to probe the emotional complexity of the man without romance or sentimentality. While the traditional adjectives applied to Peter—*impetuous, headstrong, reckless* and *stubborn*—find firm foundation in the Gospels, they threaten to reduce him to a caricature.

The reader feels that Michael Card has stepped into the trembling Peter's sandals when the terrifying splendor of Christ's divinity shines through the rags of his humanity on Mount Tabor, when the stricken apostle implores Jesus, "Depart from me, for I am a sinful man," when the unambiguous Peter confesses Jesus as the Christ, when the crushed Peter meets the eyes of his Master as the cock crows, when the spiritually intoxicated Peter is embraced by Jesus in the upper room, when the deliriously happy fisherman swims at breakneck speed to his Lord on the Tiberian seashore, when the fierce, primal energy of Peter propels him from hiding to fearlessly proclaim the risen Christ in the power of the Spirit.

Card is not a neutral, dispassionate observer when Jesus dismantles Peter's false self of inner agitation, drivenness, bravado and emotional turmoil in order to shape a new creation who will become the unquestioned leader of the apostolic community.

The eleventh-century biblical scholar and mystic Bernard of Clairvaux ("clear view") wrote, "The great quality of all the saints is humility." In the first letter of Peter, there is no trace of self bleeding through the lean and sparse verses, less narrative because the narrator was disappearing. "Wrap yourselves in humility to be servants of each other, because God refuses the proud and will always favor the humble" (1 Peter 5:5).

A Fragile Stone speaks to wobbly disciples who never seem to get it all together and to naive leaders who think they have. Michael Card has written a lyrical love song about Peter, and personally I found the melody contagious.

Brennan Manning,
author of *A Glimpse of Jesus*

Introduction

THE SEARCH FOR SIMON

I t was a glorious mid-May morning. My oldest daughter, Kate, and I were traveling together with our small music team on a tour of Romania. We had performed in Bucharest and then in Sibiu just the night before. Today, our last in the country, we were on our way to Calimanesti and finally on to the airport and home.

Our Romanian friends Emil and Romana had shown us the care and hospitality for which Romanians are known all over the world. On this, our final day together, they wanted to show us a bit of their history, the ancient Russian Orthodox monastery at Cozia.

The short walk past the souvenir stands and down the cool tree-lined lane to the monastery was a trip back in time. Back to an era before the ruthless communist dictator Nicolae Ceausescu sought to drive the Christians to extinction—long before the busyness of our own modern world started trying to choke the life from the church in another, more insidious way. Back to a time when people sought to find a holy life in seclusion, meditation and prayer, a time when time was available and could be spent listening to God.

On one wall of the entryway we saw a simple Gothic painting of two men holding up a church building between them: Peter and Paul. Peter is the characteristically robust figure of legend, wearing a somewhat uncharacteristic golden gown. Paul is the bald ball of fire we all imagine. In his hand is a bound book. He looks a bit angry or perhaps irritated standing there, as if he has somewhere else to go. Peter also looks somewhat uncomfortable, but it seems to me for a different reason. In his hand is a simple scroll. Could it be one of his two letters? As he stands there holding up one side of the building, Peter seems uncertain. I imagine him saying, "Can someone please come and take this burden away?"

This is the Simon Peter of legend, always pictured as rugged and strong, walking a few inches off the ground with the keys of the kingdom firmly in hand. He disappears as a person from the church fathers in the early third century. After that time he is only an office, simply a "chair."

I was raised with a different legend of Simon Peter. For me he was the thoroughly humanized fisherman, possessing all the foibles and fragileness of any modern man. This was the Simon Peter of the seventies—a costar in *Jesus Christ Superstar*. He was portrayed as the one who consistently had his foot in his mouth, "old impetuous Peter." He's just like you and me, only more so.

During this same period of time, I received an opposite image of him. "Peter," the preachers would intone, "the Rock, strong and solid." In this version, Jesus chose Peter because of his robust character. Simon was just the type of person for whom Jesus was looking. Even Eusebius, the first historian of the church, states that Simon was chosen for his "merits."

But all these images seemed conflicting, one-dimensional and incomplete to me. So which one was he?

Later, when Simon stepped fully formed from the pages of

A FRAGILE STONE

Acts, it was as if I had never before seen him in all my years of Bible study. He was more complex than I had ever imagined. I began to understand for the first time the wonderful progression in his character as a leader after the years of walking with Jesus. And their relationship! I had never understood just how close the two of them were, Jesus and Simon.

The Rock indeed he was. Jesus' words had proclaimed it so, and over the years of ministry he had grown by grace into the title. But he was a fragile stone still, completely dependent on his Master and Friend, even as Jesus had insisted on his own dependence on the Father. Certainly there was something solid in him, but it was Jesus' doing. And yes, he was like you and me—and again he was not. He stumbled, to be sure, lost his temper and said no to Jesus just as you and I do. But at the same time he was completely unique by virtue of the call that had been placed on his life. Sure, we all fall, but never to the degree Simon fell. And which of us will ever walk on the water?

For certain he was passionate, but not in the shallow, half-cocked way he had been portrayed to me. His was a passion that caused him to say more than he knew with a wisdom that even Jesus confessed was from heaven, or else with a foolishness so deep it could have only come from the pit. His was a passion that could murderously lash out, single-handed, against two hundred armed men. Or it could smolder, still white-hot, for the decades during which he left home and family again and again to speak Jesus' word and do his work.

In the Gospels Simon is properly the costar in the cast. He is the only other fully formed character in the Gospels besides Jesus.

In Acts, at least in the first twelve chapters, he becomes the leading man. The lovable, perpetually misunderstanding and often misunderstood disciple of the Gospels has been transformed by the Spirit into the true foundational leader of the church.

But somewhere along the way we lost him. Or perhaps it might be better to say that at several points along the way (for whatever reason) his image became blurred beyond recognition. Now we need to go back to the Scriptures to refocus and recover a truer picture.

When I began the research for this book I started by looking at my own bookshelves. There was not a single book about Peter there, though I have several on Paul's life and thought. The next morning I drove into Nashville to the Catholic bookstore, assuming it would have several books from which to choose. I thought also that it might be nice to get an icon of Peter to give me someone to talk to during the long, lonely nights of writing. I found rows of books on people like Mother Teresa and Francis of Assisi, but not a single book on Peter. And there were icons of every conceivable saint, ancient to modern, but none of Peter.

"But he's supposed to be your guy!" I prodded the young woman at the register.

Next I went confidently and arrogantly to the Protestant bookstore, assuming that they would have something helpful. But—you guessed it—nothing. It was the same at the big pagan bookstore, which, like most secular bookstores, has a large religious section situated way in the back of the store. (I'm told that a majority of their customers are looking for spiritual books or Bibles; this section is placed in the rear of the store so potential buyers will have to walk past the other shelves on the way—and find another book or two they didn't know they wanted!) Finally, I looked in a catalog and found only a few books on Peter's life. Only after extensive digging did I find a few more recently written books. All but one of these were out of print.

What is going on? I wondered. Does Peter represent such a bone of contention between the Catholics and the Protestants that everyone somehow avoids him? Is he, like Mary, "best left alone if you don't want to rock the boat"? Is he not controversial enough for the secularists? Have the Protestants become such thorough "Paulinists," as F. F. Bruce once said, that they have forsaken the rich organic contribution of Peter?

Caught Between Two Worlds

If you look at the Scriptures you'll see that Simon has always been caught between two opposing groups. In his own time he was wedged between the Jewish and Gentile Christians. It had not yet been decided whether Gentiles needed to become Jews first before they could become proper Christians. Peter would find himself, by grace, in the inspired group (along with Paul) who realized that God was doing a new work, putting new wine in new wineskins. Because of this, Peter was called before councils, arrested and hunted like a criminal because he sought to obey the One to whom he'd devoted his life those many years before.

In our own time Peter is caught between two other factions: the Catholics, who claim him as their first pope, and the Protestants, who do their best to relegate him to the Twelve with the other disciples and no more. The truth, it seems to me, is (as it usually is) somewhere in between.

The Facts of Simon's Life

Let's begin then with the simple facts of Simon's life as we have them in the New Testament:

- His given name was Simon bar-Jonah ("Simon Johnson" in modern parlance). His father's name was Jonah. We do not know his mother's name.

- He is referred to almost two hundred times in the New Testament. (The disciple John is mentioned only thirty-one times.)

- Jesus gives him the new name Peter but then mysteriously never calls him by that name.

- He has a brother, Andrew, who first brought him to Jesus (John 1:40-42). Andrew and perhaps Simon were disciples of John the Baptist (John 1:35).

- He was originally from Bethsaida, on the western coast of the Sea of Galilee (John 1:44), but relocated to Capernaum for reasons unknown to us.

- His house was large—two stories (Mark 2:4)—and provided space for Peter, his wife, his mother-in-law, his brother Andrew and possibly even Jesus (Matthew 8:14; Mark 1:29, 36; 2:2).

- He was a fisherman by trade. Along with his brother Andrew, he partnered with James and John in what is properly considered a small business (Luke 5:10).

- He was not formally educated, though like most Jewish boys he would have studied the Scriptures from the age of five (Acts 4:13).

- He was married (Matthew 8:14; Mark 1:30; Luke 4:38). (At age eighteen it would have been his duty to marry.) His wife accompanied him on at least some of his dangerous missionary trips (1 Corinthians 9:5; 1 Peter 5:13).

- He had a distinct Galilean accent, which would have sounded harsh to the rest of the people in Judea (Mark 14:70; Acts 2:7).

- He was in the core group of the twelve disciples—we could call them "the Three"—with his former fishing partners James and John (Matthew 27:56; Mark 5:37; 9:2; 14:33).

- He was clearly the leader among the Twelve. The disciples are often designated "Peter and those with him" (Mark 1:36; Luke 9:32; 8:45).

- His name always appears first in the lists of the disciples.

- He was the first to be called by name by Jesus (John 1:40-42).

- He was the first person to confess his sinfulness to Jesus.

- He receives from Jesus the most severe rebukes.

- At least seven miracles of Jesus were performed for Peter or connected to him: the two miraculous catches of fish, the curing of his mother-in-law, his walking on water, the healing of Malchus's ear, the two miraculous deliverances from prison and the coin in the fish's mouth.

- Besides Jesus, he is the central character in many of the stories in the Gospels. At the transfiguration he asks to erect "booths" (Mark 9:5). He is the only disciple to attempt walking on the water (Matthew 14:28-31). When a question arises about the temple tax, the collectors come to Peter (Matthew 17:24). The story of the footwashing is essentially a story about Peter and Jesus (John 13:1-17).

- The first Gospel (Mark) was written because of him and became the pattern for the other Synoptics, Matthew and Luke.

- Later signs of his authority from Acts and Paul's letters include these: Peter proposes the replacing of Judas (Acts 1:15-26). He preaches the first Pentecost sermon (Acts 2:14-36). He performs the first healing (Acts 3:6). He defends the gospel before the Sanhedrin (Acts 4:8-12). He decides the case of Ananias and Sapphira (Acts 5:1-11). He is the first counselor to Paul (Galatians 1:18). He mediates between James and Paul (Acts 15:5-11).

- After his miraculous release from prison (Acts 12:17), Peter leaves Jerusalem, where James takes the lead (see Acts 15; Galatians 2:9), giving himself to missionary work at Antioch, Corinth and finally Rome.

Ancient Sources on His Later Years and Death

The later years of Peter's life and ministry are not outlined in the New Testament. We must turn to ancient sources, where we find a curious tangle of probable truths and impossible myths. The following seem most likely to be true.

- Eusebius (A.D. 260-339), the first historian of the church, in *The Apostles* 2.14.25: "Hot on the heels in the same reign of Claudius, a gracious Providence brought to Rome the great and mighty Peter, chosen for his merits a leader of the other apostles. Like a noble captain of God, he proclaimed the Gospel of Light and the Word that saves souls. . . . Peter's hearers, not satisfied with a single hearing or with the unwritten teaching of the divine message, pleaded with Mark, whose Gospel we have, to leave them a written summary of the teaching given them verbally, since he was a follower of Peter. . . . So it happened that this man (Nero), the first to be announced publicly as a fighter against God, was led on to slaughter the apostles. It is related that in his reign Paul was beheaded in Rome itself and that Peter was crucified."

◆ Dionysius (A.D. 166-170), bishop of the church of Corinth, quoted in the same section by Eusebius: "By your great counsel you have bound together what has grown from the seed that Peter and Paul sowed among the Romans and Corinthians. For both of them sowed in Corinth and instructed us together; in Italy too they taught jointly in the same place and were martyred at the same time."

◆ Clement of Alexandria (c. A.D. 150-215), head of the catechetical school in Alexandria, in *Missions and Persecutions* 3.30: "Or will they reject even the apostles? For Peter and Philip had children, and Philip gave his daughters in marriage. . . . They say that when the blessed Peter saw his wife led away to death, he rejoiced that her call had come and that she was returning home."

◆ Tertullian (A.D. 155-250), a prolific Christian writer from Carthage, in *The Demurrer Against the Heretics* 36.1: "Peter endured a passion like that of the Lord."

◆ Tertullian, *Against Scorpion* 15.3: "In Rome Nero was the first to stain with blood the rising faith. Peter was girded about by another when he was made fast to the cross."

- Lactantius (A.D. 316-320), described as the Christian Cicero and tutor to the son of Constantine, in *The Deaths of the Persecutors:* "When Nero was already reigning Peter came to Rome, where, in virtue of the performance of certain miracles which he worked by the power of God which had been given to him, he converted many to righteousness and established a firm and steadfast temple to God. When this fact was reported to Nero, he noticed that not only at Rome but everywhere great multitudes were daily abandoning the worship of idols, and, condemning their old way, were going over to the new religion. Being that he was a detestable and pernicious tyrant, he sprang to the task of tearing down the heavenly temple and of destroying righteousness. It was he who first persecuted the servants of God. Peter he fixed to a cross; and Paul, he slew."

These are the New Testament facts and more probable extrabiblical aspects of Simon's life. But there is infinitely more to knowing a person than facts. We all possess an emotional and spiritual life as well, and nothing could be more evident in the biblical portrayal of Peter. Our emotional lives are expressed in the give and take of relationship as we come to know the true heart of another person, as true friendships are hammered out.

It is Peter's friendship with Jesus that we see most clearly and in the most detail in the Gospels. We read of their very first meeting, after which it seems Peter seldom left Jesus' side. The tension that sometimes flares between the two—a tension which indeed exists in any genuine and deep relationship—is seen again and again. Peter is the only one of his disciples we hear rebuking Jesus, the only person who ever says no to him. Sometimes I wonder if

Jesus didn't love him all the more for his passion. They were sometimes frustrated with each other, and yet they remained intimate friends.

When Jesus goes to struggle in Gethsemane, he takes the Three with him, but when he must come back three times to check on them, he speaks only to Peter. After the resurrection Jesus sends word, "Tell the disciples . . . and Peter." And shortly afterward Jesus first appears to Peter alone in a mysterious and unrecorded meeting.

Peter is fully himself, whatever Gospel you take up. His rich and complex character stays the same whatever Gospel you choose. He is the most human. Perhaps that's one reason Jesus seemed to be so attracted to him; indeed, it is the same reason we are still attracted to him today. It's a miracle, when you think about it, that Jesus would be able to choose a person whom so many of us could relate to, feel a kinship with and love.

Though it concerns me, I am not interested in examining what the reasons might be for Simon's disappearance from our contemporary Christian culture, but I do know I want to understand him better. After all, a great way to come closer to someone is to get to know their best friend! The depth of the friendship between Jesus and Peter is beyond question. And "at the heels of the hunt" it is Jesus I desire most deeply to know. Peter would not have it any other way.

Two Personal Notes

It may make my Protestant readers uncomfortable that I am making so much of Peter and what I see as his unquestionable primacy. Simon was the first disciple to do practically everything, from preaching to healing. Primacy also clearly implies that he was the first, the leader among the Twelve.

It may make my Catholic friends uncomfortable—perhaps even angry—that, though I will make much of the primacy of Peter, I will not be able to conclude that this leads to his supremacy. That is, I will not be able to arrive with them at the conclusion that Peter's primacy necessarily leads to his being the first pope.

I like what Oscar Cullmann says in the preface to his wonderful book on Simon Peter, *Peter: Disciple-Apostle-Martyr:* "We promote mutual and improved understanding only if we do not pass over in silence that which separates us." I am not interested in doing (or undoing) church history. But it does seem clear to me that both Catholics and Protestants have missed Peter. The Catholics have made him an office and no longer a person. The Protestants have simply denied his authority as the foundational disciple for fear of agreeing with the Catholics! I hope simply to "look for" Simon in the pages of the New Testament and honestly report to you what I discover, to better understand what Pope John Paul II called the "mystery of Peter's role in God's design for the universal church." I am also hoping and asking that my good intentions will be believed by both sides.

Second, please know that I am fully aware of the tenuousness of writing about the emotional life of someone I am separated from by two thousand years. I am willing to confess that I don't really understand my own emotional life most of the time. So why, you are justified in asking, should I embark on this journey of seeking to understand Simon Peter's emotional life?

The answer is because of the portrayal of Peter in all of the Gospels. His emotional state is so often alluded to, if not spelled out, in the text. Because this information has been provided, I believe the writers mean for us to use it in understanding who Peter is. And so, with this proviso in mind, I intend to make the most of it. I ask the reader's indulgence at many points where I will be forced to speculate. I will do my best at each point to remind you (and myself) that at that point I am just guessing. Fair enough?

As we walk through the Gospels and Acts, and reread Peter's two passionate letters, my prayer is that together we will make this journey toward a better understanding of one of the most important figures of the New Testament—but not for the sake of understanding him alone. This would have been onerous to someone like Peter. No, the ultimate reason for getting to know Peter is so together we might better know Jesus. For the story of Peter is the story of Jesus. Perhaps, if you and I do our best, the same will be said of us someday.

Part One

THE STONE

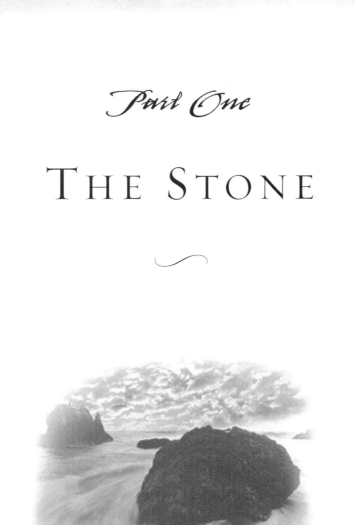

CHAPTER ONE

A Meeting on the Seashore

JOHN 1:40-43

So much of both their lives would be spent within the sight of that lake. Simon had spent most of his life on it, and the lake had given a measure of life to him. At least once it had almost taken both their lives. They would meet, and three years later, they would part ways beside this same lake, known as the "Sea of Galilee"—that body of water at the heart of green and beautiful Galilee. This was the nexus of Simon's world.

Galilee is the most fertile part of what is sometimes referred to as the "green bridge" between Asia and Africa. Major crossroads, some of the chief highways of the world in fact—roads to and from the sea, from Tyre and Sidon, the "Way of the Sea"—passed directly through Simon's homeland.

It was a good location for a small fishing business. This was the world of Simon bar-Jonah and his brother Andrew. And so it was not in the high and holy place of Jerusalem but in green and obscure Galilee that Jesus and Simon's life together began.

> Andrew, Simon Peter's brother, was one of these men who had heard what John said and then followed Jesus. The first thing Andrew did was to find his brother, Simon, and tell him, "We have found the Messiah" (which means the Christ).

> Then Andrew brought Simon to meet Jesus. Looking intently at Simon, Jesus said, "You are Simon, the son of John—but you will be called Cephas" (which means Peter). (John 1:40-42)

It is truly remarkable to me that in the Gospel of John we have a record of their very first meeting, of perhaps the first time they laid eyes on each other. Andrew is curiously identified as Peter's brother, though we have not met Peter as yet. Andrew draws near with the same confession on his lips that his brother will later become famous for affirming. Standing there, seeing for the first time the man who will become his closest friend, Peter experiences the intent gaze of Jesus. John's record uses the same Greek word here (*emblepo*) that Luke will later use to describe Jesus' piercing glance from across the high priest's courtyard when he hears Peter's final denial (Luke 22:61). But for now that scene is a world away.

John will later tell us that Jesus did not need to hear any testimony about a person. He knew what was in a person's heart and was able, before meeting them, to understand who they were (John 2:25). So what might this penetrating, understanding gaze have told Jesus about who Simon was?

Before Jesus stood what we should assume was an ordinary looking man, perhaps about his same age. No one in Scripture or any other ancient writings seems to feel the need to describe the physical appearance of either Simon or Jesus. The common device for presenting Peter in later medieval times was to show a tall, strong man with gray, curly hair and beard. He inevitably holds a ring of keys to further identify him to the largely illiterate masses that would throng to the cathedrals. But the person standing before Jesus this particular morning was centuries away from being the revered icon he would become. Like his future Friend, what is so amazing about Simon is how unamazing he is!

We might imagine what he smelled like that morning, having fished all night, as was his custom. The pungent smell of the lake mixed with his sweat and the strong smell of fish—earthy, organic, common, repelling and somehow attracting all the same, like Simon himself. He would no doubt have had a fisherman's rough hands as well, though handshaking would not become customary for another thousand years.

The understanding gaze of Jesus was not focused on the externals of the curious fisherman that morning. He looked into and saw the heart of who Simon was and what he would become.

"You *are* Simon, the son of John," Jesus said. "But you *will be* called Cephas" (John 1:42).

He was a simple fisherman, the son of a fisherman, with the most commonly given name of the day. "Simon" was the most popular name in Palestine. The Greek "Peter" was not known before the time of Tertullian in the second or third century. *Cephas,* the original Aramaic, was never known as a name. So Jesus takes a man with the most ordinary name in the land and gives him a new title. He will indeed experience a future transformation not unlike that of Abraham, for in the Bible a new name signifies a new identity, a new life.

We need to examine the new title of Simon in the context of the three separate situations in which Jesus bestows and affirms the name. Our current passage in John represents the first incident, but there are two more passages which, together with John's story, paint the entire picture. The second is found in Luke's Gospel:

> One day soon afterward Jesus went to a mountain to pray, and he prayed to God all night. At daybreak he called together all of his disciples and chose twelve of them to be apostles. Here are their names: Simon (he also called him Peter). (Luke 6:12-14; see also Mark 3:13-19)

Chosen an Apostle

We have no way of knowing how large the pool of disciples was from which Jesus finally chose the Twelve. Only Luke will tell us later of the choosing of seventy more representatives. Note that this was a special appointment, coming after the call to become a disciple (Luke 6:17). This smaller group, the Twelve, will become Jesus' *apostles,* his "sent ones," authoritative representatives speaking his word and doing his work.

It is no accident that in the above passage Luke lists Peter first among the Twelve. In every listing Peter takes the lead. Judas is always ominously named last. The future denier and the future traitor, bookends.

As all the Gospels unfold it will become clearer and clearer that beyond simply being listed first, Peter is the spokesman for the Twelve. We will see the other disciples in time discovering their corporate identity in him. Here, when Luke tells us of the choosing of the Twelve after an all-night prayer session, the future tense of John ("You will be Cephas") has become past tense ("He also called him Peter").

The first miraculous catch of fish has already taken place (Luke 5:1-11). There Peter begged Jesus to depart from him because of his sinfulness. Nevertheless, the call has come to follow, and Simon and his companions have responded. Between the first calling and the appointment as apostles, Mark records that more than ten events, mostly healings, took place. What Jesus said earlier about Simon becoming the rock has become a new, burgeoning reality in his life. The new name signifies his new mission as he is sent out with the Twelve to speak God's word and to do his work. He has been given the power, along with the others, to speak and act for Jesus, to represent him by gracious deeds and redemptive words.

And so Simon sets out with the new title he has only begun to understand. Called away from his nets and boats, from his large comfortable home in Capernaum, from his wife and her mother, from the only life he has ever known, he is plunged into a life full of daily challenges, discomforts and surprises. In newfound obedience, he pushes out into a sea of humanity to catch men and women for God.

To get the complete picture we must turn to Matthew's Gospel and the final step in the process of Simon's receiving his new identity.

Jesus replied, "You are blessed, Simon son of John, because my Father in heaven has revealed this to you. You did not learn this from any human being. Now I say to you that you are Peter, and upon this rock I will build my church, and all the powers of hell will not conquer it. And I will give you the keys of the Kingdom of Heaven. Whatever you lock on earth will be locked in heaven, and whatever you open on earth will be opened in heaven." (Matthew 16:17-19)

At this point in Matthew's Gospel we are well into the ministry of Jesus. The transfiguration of Jesus (which we will see was also a transforming moment for Simon!) is just about to take place. John the Baptist has been beheaded by Herod, and Jesus has responded by trying to get away from the crowd—no doubt for a time of grieving and reflection (Matthew 14:13). Jesus has experienced rejection in the synagogue at Capernaum. His mother and brothers have tried to apprehend him, believing he has lost his mind. The Twelve have been sent out on their first mission and have returned rejoicing. Most important, Simon has just spoken his great confession of who Jesus is.

In response, Jesus returns to the original, formal-sounding title, "Simon, son of John," the same form he used in John's account of their first meeting. He will use this formula once again, at the end of their earthly time together (John 21:15-17). Three times on the same lakeside.

"You will be . . ." "He called him . . ." And now "You are . . ." The series represents three completely different incidents, a progressive establishing of a new identity for Simon. Upon their first meeting Jesus made a promise that Simon would in the future become the rock. After some months together Jesus issued the call to become one of the Twelve. And now, because of Peter's great confession, Jesus reaffirms the new title, and (most significant) he explains precisely what it means. So what does it mean?

As we saw, Jesus made a prophetic promise when first he laid eyes on Simon. He is not yet the Rock, but how could he be? Many of us like to believe that the heart of these exchanges between Jesus and Simon had something to do with Jesus recognizing something of Simon's character. Preachers inevitably quote the first part of Matthew 16:18 and then break into the text with adjectives like *strong* or *sturdy*. But this is not a description of Simon as he is. It's what he will become.

Jesus never says, "I give you the title 'Rock' because you are so immovable and strong." The first words that come from Jesus' lips defining what *rock* means are "upon this rock *I will build*." This "rock" is simply something with which you build. Peter will be the first foundational stone in this new edifice called the church. Jesus will be the chief cornerstone (Matthew 21:42; Mark 12:10; Luke 20:17; Acts 4:11).

So Much More Than a Nickname

Often commentaries seek to explain the titling of Peter as Jesus merely bestowing a nickname, as he did when he called James and John the "sons of thunder." But Jesus is up to infinitely more. This is not simple camaraderie; it is the call. The new title contains a prophetic promise. It could have only been finally affirmed after Peter's statement of faith in who Jesus is. His confession was the necessary indication that Peter was indeed the first stone to be laid. Now that this confession has been spoken, Jesus will begin to build.

Though Jesus bestows the new title of "Rock" (*Cephas* in Aramaic), he will never call Simon by that name because it is, after all, not a proper name. He is always Simon to Jesus. Only later, in Acts, will the name Simon give way to Peter, in the same way "Christ" is a title that later became a part of Jesus' name. Jesus Christ. Simon Peter. So Peter (*Cephas*) is not merely an affectionate nickname but a prophetic title that describes who Simon will, by grace, become, a new name signifying a new life.

This is not the first time God called an ordinary man to an extraordinary future by giving him a new title. "When God looked on Abraham who was to appear, he said, 'Behold, I have found a rock on which I can build and base the world.' Therefore he called Abraham a 'rock' " (from an ancient Jewish commentary, called a *midrash,* on Isaiah 51:1-2).

"Consider . . . the rock from which you were cut . . . Abraham," Isaiah had proclaimed six hundred years before. Abram, the one who was called, renamed and given a promise that he would build a holy nation, provides the true Old Testament background for understanding the new title Simon receives.

Jesus' pronouncement concerning Simon Peter sounds hauntingly similar to the words of the rabbis when they sought to explain Isaiah's statement in their commentary. The character of Abram has nothing to do with the reference to the rock. He is not particularly strong or steadfast. In fact, the record will reveal quite the contrary. What is significant about Abram is the God who

calls him. It is all about the fact that God is building something—
a new nation—and he has graciously determined to use men and
women as building stones. The result was that the nation of Israel
eventually found their corporate identity in Abraham. Later they
would identify corporately with a series of priests and kings. All
the while God would long for them to find their identity in him.

In the same way Simon will become for the followers of Jesus
what Abraham was for Israel: a foundational leader for the community by virtue of a divine call and a confession of personal faith.
In time the disciples of Jesus will find a corporate identity in
Simon Peter. They will come to him to ask Jesus to clarify his sayings. Jesus will speak to the Twelve often by addressing only
Simon. When the tax collectors want to collect the temple tax
from Jesus, they will come and ask Simon. When the Three fall
asleep in the Garden of Gethsemane, Jesus will correct only
Simon. Not by any virtue of character or accomplishment but
solely because of the call of Jesus, Simon will serve as the repre-
sentative of the Twelve whose head and leader is always unques-
tionably Jesus.

After Jesus returns to the Father, Simon will be the vital
bridge between two disparate worlds: the world of a physically
present, perfect Leader and the other world of diverse and decidedly imperfect leaders.

Like any building, the living structure Jesus proposes to build
has a door. That door requires a key, and Peter is promised that
someday he will receive that key. Once more we are in Old
Testament territory, again in the book of Isaiah. The prophet tells
of a divine oracle who promised that his authority (symbolized by

keys) would pass to a man named Eliakim. "I will give him the key to the house of David—the highest position in the royal court. He will open doors, and no one will be able to shut them; he will close doors, and no one will be able to open them" (Isaiah 22:22).

As Simon's identity becomes solidified in Acts, we will see several instances of his "unlocking" the door of the kingdom. Through his healing people and speaking the word of Jesus, the door of the kingdom will eventually be opened to the Gentiles and to the whole world. The Pharisees, Jesus would say, "shut the kingdom of the heaven in men's faces" (Matthew 23:13 NIV). Peter and his followers would, by grace, unlock and open wide that door. The process of unlocking and opening the kingdom's doors will continue on until the end of time (Revelation 1:18; 3:7; 21:25).

But all of that lies ahead of this simple, confused fisherman. For now, he is still standing beside his familiar lake. He is holding not keys but smelly, soggy nets in chapped hands. Before him stands simply a new friend who seems to see him with understanding and sympathetic eyes. It is one of those ordinary, earth-shaking, timeless moments when two lives intersect. Simon Peter has no idea what lies ahead.

CHAPTER TWO

Jesus the Fisherman

LUKE 5:1-11

Simon rejoiced when he cast his net
And gathered in it living fish for death. . . .
Simon obeyed the One who said to him
"You have caught fish for death
(now) make disciples for life."

EPHREM THE SYRIAN, A.D. 373

One day as Jesus was preaching on the shore of the Sea of Galilee, great crowds pressed in on him to listen to the word of God. He noticed two empty boats at the water's edge, for the fishermen had left them and were washing their nets. Stepping into one of the boats, Jesus asked Simon, its owner, to push it out into the water. So he sat in the boat and taught the crowds from there.

When he had finished speaking, he said to Simon, "Now go out where it is deeper and let down your nets, and you will catch many fish."

"Master," Simon replied, "we worked hard all last night and didn't catch a thing. But if you say so, we'll try again." And this time their nets were so full they began to tear! A shout for help brought their partners in the other boat, and soon both boats were filled with fish and on the verge of sinking.

When Simon Peter realized what had happened, he fell to his knees before Jesus and said, "Oh, Lord, please leave me—I'm too much of a sinner to be around you." For he was awestruck by the size of their catch, as were the others with him. His partners, James and John, the sons of Zebedee, were also amazed.

Jesus replied to Simon, "Don't be afraid! From now on you'll be fishing for people!" And as soon as they landed, they left everything and followed Jesus. (Luke 5:1-11)

We find the two of them once again beside the lake. Peter the fisherman has been walking with Jesus the carpenter for several months now. It has been almost a year since he met Jesus (John 1:42). Mark, who records Peter's version of the story, tells of no fewer than ten events between their first meeting and this amazing moment.

When you first consider the Luke passage, you might notice what seems to be a glaring omission. Where is the sermon? Why has Luke left it out? Or could it be that Luke found a deeper lesson, not in Jesus' words but in the parable of what he did?

Jesus will never command the disciples to do something he has not first perfectly demonstrated in his own life. So if he intends to call on them to catch men, he will first show them how it is done. On this day it is Jesus who is fishing for men. He will cast his net and catch at least four, James and John, Andrew and, of course, Simon Peter.

Jesus begins by asking a favor. He asks to use one of their boats to give himself some room from the crush of the crowd—and perhaps to keep from being pushed into the lake! Using a boat for a pulpit was an imaginative way to help the disciples begin to make the transition from being fishers of fish to fishers of men. (This is not the only time Jesus will preach from a boat. See Mark 4:1.)

How could they have known that they were washing the nets for perhaps one of the last times in their lives? When Jesus is done with his sermon, he turns directly to Peter, who owns the boat, and says, "Go out to the deep water, let down your nets and you'll find a catch."

Does Jesus not know we've already fished this part of the lake and found it empty? Simon asks himself. *Doesn't he understand that we've already washed and stored the nets?* Peter, the only disciple who ever says no to Jesus, comes dangerously close this time as well. His response to Jesus is almost a no. The only reason he gives for obeying, "If you say so," will in time become the guiding principle for his life. The simple command of Jesus will eventually be all it takes to move Peter.

He has spent the last year getting to know his new Friend. Not long ago he witnessed the healing of his own mother-in-law. But now there is still a tone of reluctant obedience in Simon's voice. And then . . .

It's as if the fish have appeared from out of nowhere, as if they have been dropped into the nets from out of the blue Galilean sky. It's the kind of catch of which legends are made, a net-ripping catch! Peter calls his partners to bring the other boat over and heave to. Even with their help the boats almost sink.

"Fear Not"

In response to the miraculous catch, Peter asks for what he really does not want—he asks for Jesus to leave. He has become the frightened fish, thrashing in the net, wanting only to get away, or at least for Jesus to get away from him. Peter has come face to face with the frightening possibility of complete success. Failure, like their earlier empty nets, seems so much safer and predictable.

We will see later that often in the presence of Peter, when Jesus reveals his true nature in a new way, the first words from his lips are "Don't be afraid." When he calms the storm (Mark 4:40), when he walks on the water (Mark 6:50; John 6:20), when he is transfigured into blazing light (Matthew 17:7) and when he is raised from the dead (Matthew 28:10)—each time Jesus comforts and calms Peter with these words. In each instance, when the veil is momentarily lifted and Peter has the terrifying realization that he, a veteran sinner, is in the presence of undiminished Deity, it totally undoes him (as indeed it should). Have you ever come close enough to be terrified by the glory of Jesus?

But to be told "Don't be afraid" in each of the above incidents makes some sense. In the middle of the storm, when the disciples could taste the fear in their mouths, it was the perfect thing to say. So too, when they thought they had seen a ghost, "Don't be afraid" was what they most needed to hear. Likewise, seeing the unveiled glory of Jesus must have struck terror in their sleepy hearts. In one moment to see their simple familiar friend standing alone and the next moment to be blinded be the radiance that they now knew had always been there, just under the surface of his humanity, would cause an awe-filled fear.

But what's so terrifying about a net full of fish? Though this kind of volume was certainly a rarity for Simon and his partners, they had seen lots of fish before. Even the miraculous fact that they had come from out of nowhere, out of a lake they knew was empty, is an occasion for wonder certainly, but fear?

Simon fears because he is a man who, thanks to the preaching of John the Baptist, has become aware of his sinful state. And now he has become the beneficiary of Jesus, who has graciously filled his nets in spite of himself. There was nothing in his experience, nor in ours, that could have prepared him for this kind of frightening generosity. We are forever asking for the things we think we deserve. Simon knew then what we need to learn now: what we *deserve* is only death and separation from God and all his goodness. If we, for one blink, could step back and glimpse the awesome generosity of the One who should, by all rights, destroy us, we would join Simon on our knees with the same confession on our trembling lips.

Fear is what has driven Simon to his knees. He has heard the preaching of John the Baptist: "Repent, for the kingdom is at hand." His heart has been preconditioned by that preaching; he has been pricked by an awareness that he is, in fact, not ready for the kingdom's coming. We should all be rightly afraid for the whole world to be on fire. But now, behold, it has so obviously come. Jesus' miracle language provides the perfect message for the fishermen. You speak to Magi with a star. You convince a fisherman with fish! What he has waited, prayed and longed for all his life is *here!* And the thought of it absolutely scares Simon to death. The overflowing nets are the sign.

Jesus' word is crucial. "Fear not!" Our sinfulness will ultimately be dealt with. Now, because of his coming, our sin can never stand between us and Jesus. Peter's confession of his sinfulness means he is precisely the man for whom Jesus is looking. In fact, he is the first person to confess his sinfulness to Jesus.

"They must burn their boats and plunge into absolute insecurity in order to learn the demand and the gift of Christ" (Bonhoeffer, *The Cost of Discipleship,* p. 53).

Jesus has come, and the line between the worlds of the Old Testament and the New is now clearly drawn in the sand beside the lake. In the world of the Old Testament, having faith meant waiting faithfully for God to make good on his promises. In the New Testament world, faith means only one thing: following Jesus. Not only did the four of them walk away from their nets and boats, they left behind a net full of fish to follow Jesus! The promises have all been fulfilled; the Promised One is here. Now having faith means following the One in whom God has spoken his "Yes!" to every pledge he ever made to us. The fishermen really have no choice: if they are to be faithful, they must follow. We too really have no choice. Waiting is no longer an option.

If we are to be honest, we'll admit that to follow—to really leave everything behind—is an absolutely terrifying prospect. Our most natural response would be, like Peter, to fall down and say,

"Go away! This is more than I can deal with. I couldn't be the person you're looking for."

We stand before these terrifying possibilities—to let go of our security, to open ourselves to the frightening possibility of complete and utter success, to leave all that is familiar and safe for an unknown world. But then we notice that standing beside us is Jesus. He confidently whispers, "Don't be afraid. Let go of the nets. Do not be afraid. After all, it's me." Jesus has shown Simon that the sea he thought was empty was in fact full of fish. And Simon has begun to learn what it means to become partners with Jesus. A new kind of fishing lies ahead.

There comes a point in our lives when all the pieces of our past, both good and bad, come together to make a meaningful whole. It came for Peter at this point. All this time he had been fishing for fish, with varying success. Now Jesus tells him it is men and women he will be fishing for, and it makes such complete and perfect sense to Peter that he simply walks away from his old life and embraces the unknown new. Jesus, the carpenter from Nazareth, was also, it seems, a fisherman. And it was Simon Peter who got caught that day.

CHAPTER THREE

A Glimpse Inside His Household

LUKE 4:38-39

*After leaving the synagogue that day, Jesus went to Simon's home,
where he found Simon's mother-in-law very sick with a high fever. "Please
heal her," everyone begged. Standing at her bedside, he spoke to the fever,
rebuking it, and immediately her temperature returned to normal.
She got up at once and prepared a meal for them*

LUKE 4:38-39

How does one make the leap from knowing of someone merely as a historical character to seeing him or her as a real person? There was, after all, an actual living, breathing man named Simon, with a wife and a house that needed repairs (especially if the house with the hole in its roof was Peter's; see Mark 1:29; 2:1-4). There are ancient stories of at least one child, a crippled daughter, Petronella.

He paid his taxes. He worried about the details of his business. He had aches and pains and prejudices and fears—yes, fears.

He lived in Capernaum, "the village of Nahum." A very reliable tradition identifies the site of his house, precisely eighty-four feet south of the synagogue. (What kind of person buys a house one door down from the synagogue?) On this spot there was once a large, two-story house consisting of several rooms clustered around a large courtyard. Excavators have found several fishhooks in the rubble! If this really is Peter's home, it was the scene of so many of those early gatherings "at the door" (Mark 1:33; 2:1-3).

The remains of it are still there. In the fourth century someone built a large wall around it, to separate the structure from the rest of the town. In the fifth century Byzantine Christians built an octagonal basilica over the site, just as they did at Bethlehem over the birthplace of Jesus. In the seventh century, Muslim invaders destroyed the church as well as everything else in Capernaum. Today a modern sanctuary is there, straddling the ruins of the earlier ancient church as well as what is left of the original house.

Assuming this was actually Peter's house, those walls would have quite a story if only they could talk (that is, if they were still standing)! Imagine all that happened under that roof! That simple structure became the base of operations for Jesus' ministry in Galilee. Imagine him coming and going, perhaps having his own room, the only room he would ever call his own. Mark (who records Peter's account of the story of Jesus) hints that Jesus might have even called it his home! It was there that the paralytic was healed. It was within those walls that Jesus first confronted the disciples when they had been arguing about who was the greatest (Mark 9:33). Some scholars believe that the child Jesus used as an example to rebuke them might even have been Peter's own daughter! Think of all that went on within that cluster of rooms, the times of meal fellowship, the long discussions in simple, plain-spoken Aramaic with their thick Galilean dialect—arguments, laughter, prayer and singing.

For the second time now Jesus meets Peter at the point of his need. First there was the miracle catch. Now, after they make the eighty-four-foot journey home from the synagogue service, they find his mother-in-law has become seriously ill. This is not an inconvenient bout of the flu. In the first century such a high fever could spell life or death.

Simon had only recently accepted the call to follow Jesus. Now, so early in their walk together, Satan seeks to discourage him and disrupt his home. Did Simon ask himself if this was the reward for following Jesus, finding his mother-in-law in bed with what doctor Luke informs us is a "high-grade" fever? Would he have grumbled, "Is this what I get for giving my life to him?" I would have.

By all tenets of the culture, she should not have been there in the first place. If her husband was still alive she should have been living with him. If not, one of her living sons was obliged to take her in. If she had no husband or sons her own family was supposed to care for her. We can only speculate, but her presence in the house hints at an openness in Peter not only to care for his wife but to take on this extra burden for love.

Luke tells us that Jesus "rebuked" the fever. That is, he spoke directly to it, telling "it" to leave, which of course "it" had no choice but to do. There is no recovery time, no word of Jesus telling someone to bring her something to eat as he later does with the little girl he raises. No, immediately she gets up and does for Jesus what she no doubt did for every visitor to that home, what she would have done for you or me if we could have visited there. She served them the special evening Sabbath meal. This is the only Sabbath healing I can think of that did not get Jesus into trouble, probably because it occurred in the privacy of Simon's house.

What effect did the presence of such a woman have on Peter and his household? Granted, we have only the most meager scrap of evidence, but her immediate and selfless servanthood speaks clearly of the tone she would have set in the home. It hints to us as well about what kind of woman Peter had taken as his bride—of the imprint of the mother on the daughter who became the wife. The old saying is true, "When you marry a woman you're marrying her mother as well." Peter's house was a home where hospitality was practiced, not because it was dictated by the culture, but because it came freely and easily to the two women of the house, to the mother and the daughter.

I cannot help but believe that when he wrote in the third chapter of his first letter about what makes a woman truly beautiful, it was his own wife and perhaps her mother he had in mind. The images of the "purity and reverence" of their lives were alive in his mind, the "unfading beauty" of their "gentle and quiet" spirits.

It is all we will ever be able to guess about the character of his wife, of the woman who Paul informs us would later suffer with him on dangerous mission trips (1 Corinthians 9:5). Later sources tell us she was martyred just before her famous husband. As Peter witnessed her being led off to die, the legend says, he shouted a word of encouragement to her, his bride, the mother of his child, the keeper of his home, eighty-four feet south of the synagogue. "Remember the Lord!" he is said to have called out as she went to her death.

CHAPTER FOUR

The Fearless Water Walker

MATTHEW 14:22-33

Immediately after this, Jesus made his disciples get back into the boat and cross to the other side of the lake while he sent the people home. Afterward he went up into the hills by himself to pray. Night fell while he was there alone. Meanwhile, the disciples were in trouble far away from land, for a strong wind had risen, and they were fighting heavy waves.

About three o'clock in the morning Jesus came to them, walking on the water. When the disciples saw him, they screamed in terror, thinking he was a ghost. But Jesus spoke to them at once. "It's all right," he said. "I am here! Don't be afraid."

Then Peter called to him, "Lord, if it's really you, tell me to come to you by walking on water."

"All right, come," Jesus said.

So Peter went over the side of the boat and walked on the water toward Jesus. But when he looked around at the high waves, he was terrified and began to sink.

"Save me, Lord!" he shouted.

Instantly Jesus reached out his hand and grabbed him. "You don't have much faith," Jesus said. "Why did you doubt me?" And when they climbed back into the boat, the wind stopped.

Then the disciples worshiped him. "You really are the Son of God!" they exclaimed. (Matthew 14:22-33; see also Job 9:8, 11)

On two separate occasions we see the disciples caught out in the Sea of Galilee. The first incident is the occasion of a violent storm. Mark tells us that the boat was almost swamped by it (Mark 4:37). He portrays the storm as a demonic attack. Jesus shouts to the storm the same command we hear him shouting to the demon-possessed: "Be muzzled!" Luke refers to the storm as a squall, a line of violent wind, thunder and lightning (Luke 8:23).

Matthew and Mark both tell of a second incident. In this story the disciples are caught in a strong wind, not a full-blown storm. Mark tells us they were straining against the oars, for the wind was against them.

But the difference between the two accounts is not the condition of the weather. The major difference is that in the first story Jesus is with them in the boat, though he is asleep. In this second account, the one before us now, he is nowhere to be seen.

Both Matthew and Mark tell us that Jesus, after he dismissed the crowd, had gone into the hills to pray. Only Mark's account (informed by Peter) gives us the detail that Jesus could see the disciples in their difficult situation. Both writers tell us Jesus left his prayers and walked on the water to be with his men. If they are caught in a struggle, he wants to be there with them.

It was almost dawn, the fourth or last watch of the night. Only Peter gives us the mystifying detail that Jesus was about to pass by them. When they all saw him, walking on the water, they drew what, if you think about it, was a fairly logical conclusion. They thought they were seeing a ghost. What else would walk on the water in the middle of such a scary, windy night?

Jesus walking on the sea is a divine revelation of who he is. He has just fed the five thousand, revealing himself to be the "prophet like Moses" (Deuteronomy 18). As the people received the bread some of them began to murmur, "Could this be the prophet (like Moses)?" Although we will later see that the disciples had missed the connection, at least some of the people in the crowd had begun to understand. Now Jesus walks on the water. He is more than the "manna provider"; he is Deity. Mark's detail that he was "passing by" hearkens back to Exodus 33:22, when God revealed himself to Moses by placing him in the cleft of the rock and causing his glory to "pass by." Walking on the water was an undeniable demonstration of what Job 9:8 speaks about:

> He alone has spread out the heavens and marches on
> the waves of the sea.

An unnamed psalmist seems to have prophetically gazed at this very incident. He writes in Psalm 107:23-29:

Some went off in ships,

> plying the trade routes of the world.

They, too, observed the LORD's power in action,

> his impressive works on the deepest seas.

He spoke, and the winds rose,

> stirring up the waves.

Their ships were tossed to the heavens

> and sank again to the depths;

> the sailors cringed in terror.

They reeled and staggered like drunkards

> and were at their wits' end.

"LORD, help!" they cried in their trouble,

> and he saved them from their distress.

He calmed the storm to a whisper

> and stilled the waves.

Like so many other incidents in the life of Jesus, this moment is wrapped in the Old Testament. The climax of the revelation comes when Jesus literally calls out, "I am." He speaks the personal name of God, the name by which the Lord revealed himself to Moses in Exodus 3:14.

Here again it helps to keep in mind that this is the second instance of the disciples in distress at sea. Peter remembers the former angry storm and Jesus' rebuke, "How is it that you have no faith?" He is determined now that he will not hear those words again from Jesus (Mark 4:35-41). "If it is you," he says, "tell me to come to you on the water."

What sort of person wants to walk on the water in the middle of a dark windstorm? Was he motivated by some innate desire to do what he saw Jesus doing? Or did he want to walk on the water simply so he could be with Jesus? Whatever the reason, Peter often wants to do the wrong thing for the right reason. The peculiarly worded question shows that he is beginning to understand that it is only the call of Jesus that will make the impossibility of walking on the water possible. With all that he doesn't know, Simon somehow does understand that the call must originate with Jesus. This explains the clumsy wording of his request. "If it's you, tell me to come to you," he shouts above the howling wind. Bonhoeffer says that discipleship is never an offer we make to Christ. It is only the call of Jesus that makes everything possible.

All of us sometimes ask to do things that we do not have the faith to do. Was Peter's request courage or insanity or a little bit of both? the courage and the foolishness of faith? What often goes unappreciated is the fact that Peter's short walk was indeed a triumph of faith. It is his first miracle! Was this not an astounding experiment?

But then something about the experiment went terribly wrong. Peter looked around at reality and began to do what he should have naturally done under the influence of gravity when he first climbed down out of the boat: he began to sink. In the very midst of the miracle he doubts the new reality he has just stepped into, and it all starts to unravel. He apparently had no doubt when he stepped out on the water. He asked for no proof beyond the sound of Jesus' command to come to him. Without proof he walked on the water. When he saw the waves, he began to need proof that the impossible he was doing could somehow be possible. But what proof could there be that the impossible had become possible besides actually doing the impossible?

There is no proof great enough to prevent doubt. If you base your belief on proof, sooner or later you too will sink! Notice that the earlier "if" of his first request disappears. He does not say, "If you can save me"—he just yells, "Save me, Lord!" Peter finds Jesus' hand is immediately there, saving him, holding him up. The rebuke he and the others received in the middle of the first storm, "Have you no faith?" is softened. "You of little faith," Jesus says as the wind whips at his beard, "why did you doubt?"

Why did Peter doubt? After all, he had begun to accomplish it, he had walked on the water. But there was a deeper lesson he had to learn, and Jesus is intent on him not missing it, even as now you and I must learn it if we are to move forward as we walk through the wind storm of following Jesus. It is almost never heard in American churches. Indeed there are some congregations who would call it heresy. The lesson is that Peter needed to sink in order to take the next step of faith in Jesus. Because walking on the water does not ultimately increase our faith, only sinking does! Those who ask for miracles and receive them soon forget. But those who suffer for Christ's sake never forget. They have their own wounds to remind them. When we are hurting we do not flee to the rich and healthy for wisdom and real comfort. We seek out those who have fellowshiped in the sufferings of Jesus.

Jesus and the half-soaked Peter climb into the boat, and the wind, as if exhausted as well, dies down. And then something even more extraordinary occurs. Up till this time in Matthew's Gospel, Jesus has been worshiped by the Magi, by a leper and by a ruler of the synagogue. At the first storm the disciples wondered, "Who is this man?" Now they have begun to know. We have never heard or seen the disciples worshiping him until this moment. "Truly you are the Son of God!" they confess. The cumulative weight of all the revelation—the feeding of the five thousand, walking on the water and now the calm Jesus' presence provides after the windstorm—have convinced the disciples of his real identity.

Mark, in his account, does not tell us about their worship. He speaks of their complete amazement over Jesus. The reason he gives is the hardness of their hearts. He looks back at the feeding of the five thousand and lets us in on a secret: the disciples had not understood about the loaves. Not until they saw Jesus walking on the water did they put it all together. The feeding and the walking on the water are linked. They were both crucial manifestations of the true nature of Jesus, of his oneness with the Father. When the disciples finally understood, they worshiped him.

An Amazing Exclusion

There is one more striking difference between Peter's account of this story and Matthew's, an amazing exclusion. In Mark, Peter makes no mention whatsoever of his walking on the water. Before I began seeking to understand his heart, I would have thought the reason for the omission was his failure. He had begun to sink. I believed the absence of the story in his account was an indication of his immaturity and pride. Now that he has begun to come into focus for me, now that I have looked at the whole of his life and have begun to see who he became, I believe Peter left out the story not because he sank but because he walked. It was not pride but humility that kept him from mentioning his miraculous though interrupted feat.

The story is a real-life parable of the cycle of faith. We all walk sometimes and sink sometimes as well. We all cry out, "Go away from me, I'm a sinful person!" and in the next breath shout, "Come and save me!" Most of all, we all struggle with the perceived realities of the fallen world over against the unseen certainty of the kingdom.

Peter, after all, is a realist. He is you and me, at our best and at our worst. And that is why we love him like we do, at least when we finally take the time to know him. Jesus will never condemn Peter, or us, for looking at reality. The waves and the wind are real. The smell coming from Lazarus' tomb is real. When I

The Egyptian hieroglyphic for "impossible."

look at the world I will always have reason to doubt. Gravity, cancer, poverty—they are all real. But Jesus continually calls to Peter—and to you and me—to look somehow beyond all that, to a new reality where walking on the water is also real, and feeding thousands of people with a few crumbs, and rising from the dead. And we are never to doubt this impossible new reality, even as we are taking part in it.

The world that Peter and you and I are being called to exit has a million confusing faces: our fragile health, hunger, our fallen situation, the aching loneliness of the world. The world Jesus calls us into has but one focus: him! When Peter looks only at the face of Jesus, he begins to rise toward that new world, the world of the kingdom.

There is one certain way to know if you've had a brush with that other impossible new world. You will find yourself doing what the disciples did when they got Jesus back into their boat: you will find yourself worshiping him. Worship is the language of our new reality. But we must never forget that it always begins with a cry for help. It *always* begins that way. It ends when we find ourselves doing the unreal and impossible, when we discover that we, if even for a moment, have risen above the noise of the wind and the confusion of the waves. We find in the darkness a Face. We discover in the tumult a Hand. And we worship him for it all.

CHAPTER FIVE

Who They Both Are

MATTHEW 16:13-23

Not two minutes ago my best friend, Scott, came by to see me. Being a pastor, his day is unbelievably busy. As we talked together for a few minutes, he looked at his watch and realized he had a meeting coming up soon. Nevertheless, he sat down beside the fire and asked me where I was on this manuscript. He listened to new ideas I was excited about. Above all, in the midst of what is always a painful, doubt-filled process, he encouraged me. He spoke in specifics about other books I had written that had been helpful to him. In essence he came because he knew I needed to hear someone say I could do this.

There was a time, twenty-five years ago, when I did something like that for him. He was frustrated writing and recording music and being on the road away from his growing family. Everywhere we went Scott could always connect at a deep level, comforting and encouraging people. He was obviously gifted far beyond the simple ability to write and sing songs.

That evening in the church parking lot, I said something like, "So many people can do the music—so few have the gifts you have. You are a pastor." He gave a deep sigh. He had been waiting for years to have someone confirm what he knew in his heart was true about himself. What's more, he needed someone close to understand and appreciate the deeper value of what he was being called to.

We have been close friends now for twenty-five years. This friendship is stable; neither of us is going anywhere. Our plan is to someday sit on the square in Franklin, Tennessee, and count out-of-state license plates. Two little old men, characters.

Friends help each other understand who the other is. They define one another over the course of a lifetime.

Who Am I?

We leap now almost to the end of the story. They have been together at least two years by now. The cross is little more than six months away. There have been any number of miracles and signs that clearly point to who Jesus is. The Twelve should understand his true nature by now. Yet Peter remembers and tells Mark that shortly before this incident, Jesus was still forced to ask them, "Do you still not understand?" (Mark 8:21). The time is drawing near, is drawing short. A crisis is upon them.

> When Jesus came to the region of Caesarea Philippi, he asked his disciples, "Who do people say that the Son of Man is?"
>
> "Well," they replied, "some say John the Baptist,

some say Elijah, and others say Jeremiah or one of the other prophets."

Then he asked them, "Who do you say I am?"

Simon Peter answered, "You are the Messiah, the Son of the living God."

Jesus replied, "You are blessed, Simon son of John, because my Father in heaven has revealed this to you. You did not learn this from any human being. Now I say to you that you are Peter, and upon this rock I will build my church, and all the powers of hell will not conquer it. And I will give you the keys of the Kingdom of Heaven. Whatever you lock on earth will be locked in heaven, and whatever you open on earth will be opened in heaven." Then he sternly warned them not to tell anyone that he was the Messiah.

From then on Jesus began to tell his disciples plainly that he had to go to Jerusalem, and he told them what would happen to him there. He would suffer at the hands of the leaders and the leading priests and the teachers of religious law. He would be killed, and he would be raised on the third day.

But Peter took him aside and corrected him. "Heaven forbid, Lord," he said. "This will never happen to you!"

Jesus turned to Peter and said, "Get away from me, Satan! You are a dangerous trap to me. You are seeing things merely from a human point of view, and not from God's." (Matthew 16:13-23)

All of the Synoptics (Matthew, Mark and Luke) report that the confession of Peter occurred in the beautiful region around Caesarea Philippi. (Compare the Matthew passage with Mark 8:27-30 and Luke 9:18-21.) It is highly significant that the transfiguration will happen next, on the nearby slopes of Mount

Hermon. It is vital to see that the confession came before the revelation, not the other way around.

But there were other associations with this place that make me wonder if perhaps Jesus had come here specifically to give his disciples a chance to make their profession.

Caesarea Philippi was the site of the ancient city of Paneas. The name of the city was derived from the god Pan. A limestone cave was there containing an altar where the pagan deity was worshiped by Syrian Greeks. Later Herod the Great would change the name of the town in honor of Augustus Caesar. There he would build a temple where Augustus would be worshiped as a god. The temple was near the grotto of Pan. The area was no doubt filled with pagan associations for both Jesus and his disciples. In light of the surroundings, this is the perfect place to hear the affirmation that it is neither Pan nor Augustus but Jesus who is the Son of the living God.

Luke tells us Jesus had been praying in a private place before the discussion with his disciples (9:18). Matthew simply says he asked, "Who do people say the Son of Man is?" Jesus has consistently referred to himself by means of this prophetic title. There is clearly no confusion among the disciples as to the fact that he is referring to himself.

It is important to realize that Jesus is not asking the question to gain information. John has made it clear that Jesus does not need to ask people questions (John 2:24-25). He is, in fact, offering the disciples an opportunity to confess who they believe him to be. His asking should be seen as the granting of an opportunity to take the next step in their faith and understanding of who he is. It is important as well that he begins by asking what others are saying about who he is.

This is one of the few times the disciples will speak for themselves. They respond with the same confused list we already read in Mark 6:14. Some (namely Herod) thought Jesus was John the Baptist come to life again. This was clearly an erroneous point of view since Jesus and John had been contemporaries. Some believed Jesus might be the Elijah who was to come before the return of the Messiah. This reflects an understanding of the very last promise made in the Old Testament, from Malachi 4:5:

> Look, I am sending you the prophet Elijah before the great and dreadful day of the LORD arrives.

But Jesus had already identified John the Baptist as the one who had fulfilled that prophecy (Matthew 11:14). Finally, some in the crowd believed Jesus was Jeremiah or one of the prophets. Clearly the crowd was confused. (John will make this point abundantly clear in his Gospel.) What seems most important to Jesus at this present moment is not the confusion of the crowd but the understanding of the disciples.

"But what about you?" Jesus asks.

Here, as in so many other places, Peter speaks for the Twelve. Had he not opened his mouth, the pain of the silence would have been unbearable for everyone, especially Jesus. Peter is the first to experience what Kierkegaard would describe two thousand years later: "In order to fully understand what it means to be a Christian, you must stand in the crowd, point to a man and say, 'He is God.' " There is a barely perceptible but highly significant shift in the tone of Peter's reply. He does not directly answer the question as Jesus asked it. That is, he does not preface his statement with the words "We say you are . . ." Instead, he openly and forcefully confesses the fact, "You are the Christ, the Son of the Living God."

In spite of his strict Jewish monotheism, Peter is willing to ascribe divinity to Jesus. To say he is God's Son is to suggest that he is God. What an incredible leap of faith this took!

Remember Jesus' original question, "Who do people say the Son of Man is?" Peter's response is clear. The Son of Man is the Son of God! This has become the basis for the church's confession for two thousand years. It remains one thing we all seem to be able to agree on.

Like so many other times, Peter has spoken more than he knows, more than he yet understands. Yet Jesus pronounces a *barocha* or rabbinic blessing on him for his response. He reverts to the formal title "son of Jonah," which he reserves for important announcements at significant moments in Peter's life. "Blessed are you." Jesus announces, "This was not revealed to you by man . . ." Certainly this is clear. All that human wisdom could offer at this point was the confused list the disciples had mouthed before about who Jesus was. If the truth were to be spoken, God would have to speak it, as indeed he had at the baptism of Jesus. Now he has graciously chosen to speak through the fragile stone that is Simon, the son of Jonah. The confession is not to be understood as an achievement by Peter. It is all God's doing, speaking through his servant.

Then the exchange takes a remarkable turn. Jesus has asked the disciples to tell him who he is. Peter has answered on behalf of the Twelve by means of divine revelation. Now, in parallel form, Jesus will tell Peter who *he* is.

You Are Peter

"You are Peter," Jesus echoes back. It is the title, the promise he spoke when he first laid eyes on Simon. It is the name he affirmed when he called him to be a disciple. Now, in light of Simon's confession, he will explain what the title will come to mean.

"On this rock I will build my church." The preponderance of scholars, both Protestant and Catholic, have concluded that "this rock" must refer to Peter himself. The parallelism is clear. And this is, of course, the central verse on which the Catholic Church rests its understanding of the supremacy of Peter. As I tried to make clear in the introduction, I do not intend to dispute that interpretation. I would, however, like to suggest a different way of reading it. This approach stresses the primacy, not the supremacy, of Peter. In this view the rock is clearly still Peter himself. He is seen to be the very first, the primary, and the foundational stone of the church that Jesus has now, for the first time in his ministry, spoken about.

Simon has not somehow won the title by his superior insight. In just a moment he will betray his lack of understanding and speak, in almost the same breath, on behalf of Satan. No, by grace, God has chosen to speak the truth about his Son through Peter. Jesus, in his graciousness, blesses Peter for what he is not ultimately responsible for. This will be the pattern of his and all the disciples' service for Jesus for the rest of their lives, as it remains ours today. Jesus begins to build the church on the first person who, by faith, confesses who he is. Millions will follow through the ages. Peter's first confession is still unique and unrepeatable by virtue of the fact that it was the first. Jesus is only following his own advice in Luke 6:48. Any wise builder builds his house on a rock.

Jesus goes on to expand the call of Peter by promising that he will give him the keys of the kingdom, to bind and to loose. Again, Peter is the first to receive this commission from Jesus. His primacy is unquestionable. But Jesus will extend this authority to the other disciples in Matthew 18:18.

> Truly I say to you, whatever you bind on earth shall have been bound in heaven; and whatever you loose on earth shall have been loosed in heaven. (NASB)

After a lifetime of ministry Peter will reflect back and reveal just how he understands his unique and primary position. In his first letter he writes:

> Come to Christ, who is the living cornerstone of God's temple. He was rejected by the people, but he is precious to God who chose him.
> And now God is building you, as living stones, into his spiritual temple. What's more, you are God's holy priests, who offer the spiritual sacrifices that please him because of Jesus Christ. (1 Peter 2:4-5)

In his unquestionable humility, Peter sees the title "rock" as inclusive. He does not clutch the name to himself as if he were the greatest. No, he painfully learned that lesson when he was with Jesus. In his mind you and I are living stones as well. He was the first. We have followed after him. Augustine said, "For it was not one man but the unity of the Church which received the keys. . . . When to him it was said, 'I hand over to you,' what was in fact handed over was handed over to all" (*Sermons* 6.1526).

We will pick up the story in the next chapter. But for now it is enough to say that from this point on in the ministry of Jesus, a new vision for what the word *Messiah* means will dominate. Upon the confession of Peter it has been established among the Twelve that Jesus is indeed the Messiah. From this point on Jesus will struggle to make them understand what the term *Messiah* really means. And as always is the case, the struggle will begin with Peter.

If Jesus can be said to have had a best friend, it was certainly Simon Peter. It has been my experience that friends define each other. When I am uncertain about the direction of my life, I go to my closest friends to affirm, or perhaps reaffirm, who I am and what the calling on my life is all about.

What we see between Simon and Jesus is not unlike that. Certainly Jesus does not need to be told who he is. But perhaps in his humanity there was still from time to time the hunger for the assurance of his friend. And beyond a doubt Peter needed the defining presence of Jesus in his life, as we all do. As Peter's circle of friends expands with his ministry, we will see him doing the same thing in his letters. Again and again, he writes telling us who we are: strangers, a royal priesthood, God's elect. That is what friends do. They help each other understand who they are. Jesus and Peter are both rocks in their own unique ways—Jesus, forever the solid Rock (Psalm 18:31; Isaiah 26:4; 44:8); Simon, always (but by grace) the fragile stone. In the intimacy of their sometimes volatile friendship they will strive to reflect the truth of who they are to each other for the short amount of time they have left.

If you are the sort of person who usually reads books like this, you would no doubt confess that Jesus is your friend. If that is true, then my question is, "How does he define you?" He began defining us all when he told us we were sinners. Then he gave us a hunger to know him, and we followed. But how long ago was that? And in the meantime, what has the complexion of your friendship looked like?

In Revelation 2:17 he hints at the fact that someday he will give us a white stone with a new name, our new name. Perhaps for Simon his was Peter, and Jesus simply could not wait to let him know. But what do you think your name might be? What will he call you? What will he call me?

CHAPTER SIX

Loyal Despair

JOHN 6:53-71

The true test of discipleship is following Jesus not when the crowd is along for the ride but following him when no one else sees any sense in following him at all.

When I was in college my sister Caroline experienced one of the most severe tests of faith I have ever witnessed. In a thirteen-month period two of her children died, both infants who were born full term and lived only about two months. The first had multiple birth problems. When it went home to be with the Lord, though it was painful for us, we could see God's merciful hand in it all. The second came thirteen months later. It was perfect. A beautiful child. Within two months it also died, this time of a ruptured appendix. None of us saw this coming. As a family we did our best to hold together through it all. But we didn't do it well. Each of us grieved individually in such a way that we gradually drifted apart, most of all my sister and her husband.

I remember going out in the field behind the place where I was living and literally shaking my fist at God. "If this is the sort of thing you do, I don't want any part of you!" I screamed through my tears. Despair—the sin that leads to all other sin.

In time we mostly sorted out our individual struggles. In time my brother and his wife would lose an eighteen-year-old son to cancer. And the heart of our family tore a little bit more. I came to realize that Jesus is the Stumbling Stone, the Scandalon. I poured my understanding into a recording and then went about the country telling everyone the message I was still barely able to understand.

Of the two confessions of Peter, the one given in John's Gospel is important because it is spoken in a context of just such despair. One of the features of John's Gospel that sets it apart from Matthew, Mark and Luke is its tendency to leave out significant sections and stories from the life of Jesus and substitute new information. A full 92 percent of the Gospel of John is completely new and unique. That is one reason we love it the way we do. The passage before us represents one of John's most interesting omissions and most meaningful substitutions.

We left off, in the previous Synoptic section, as Jesus was about to confront Peter. In Matthew's extended account Jesus has begun to explain what it means to be the Christ. For Peter as well as the other disciples, it clearly implies a throne and eternal glory for Jesus. What Peter does not understand is that before the glory there must come the Passion, the suffering and death of the Christ.

Peter should not be looked down on for his naiveté. All the disciples—in fact, practically everyone in Judea—believed the same. They were the products of the popular teaching of the Pharisees who said that the Christ would not suffer. All of the prophetic passages in the Old Testament that speak of the suffering of Jesus (called the "suffering servant of the Lord" passages, Psalm 22; 69; Isaiah 53) the Pharisees applied to themselves. In their minds they were the Lord's suffering servants. How could the Messiah ever possibly experience suffering? It defied all human logic. But Jesus always did and always will.

Consequently, when Jesus begins to define his messiahship in terms of death and the cross, Peter takes him aside and rebukes him. "This will never happen to you!" he blurts out as he tries to imagine the unimaginable. That is Satan's great hope, of course, that Jesus will not go to the cross, will not suffer for the sins of the world. And so for the moment Peter has become Satan's dark spokesman.

Then Jesus makes a remarkable statement to Simon, the Rock. "You are a stumbling stone to me," he counters. And in so saying he applies to Peter an idea that we might have thought applied only to Jesus, the Scandalon, the stone of stumbling. (See also 1 Peter 2:7.)

They are both rocks, after all. Jesus has pronounced Peter to be such. And throughout the Old and New Testaments Jesus is called the Rock as well (Isaiah 8:14; 1 Corinthians 10:4).

But now it is Peter who is scandalizing Jesus, who is tempting him to stumble in the one area that matters most, his perfect obedience to the Father. Again, Peter says something to Jesus that we never hear anyone else say: "No!" Jesus responds with the most severe words he ever speaks to anyone and turns his former blessing into a curse. "Get behind me, Satan."

We too can be either a living stone or a stumbling block. And the awful truth is that we can sometimes be both at once.

In the Synoptic accounts we just examined, Jesus had only recently fed the four thousand. The story in John, which we will now look at, came at a later time in the ministry and at a completely different place. We clearly have two different events being portrayed in the Synoptics and John. The link between the two is that they both represent a confession of Peter. We will examine the Johannine passage now because its context of despair needs to be understood first.

> Even his disciples said, "This is very hard to understand. How can anyone accept it?"
>
> Jesus knew within himself that his disciples were complaining, so he said to them, "Does this offend you? Then what will you think if you see me, the Son of Man, return to heaven again? It is the Spirit who gives eternal life. Human effort accomplishes nothing. And the very words I have spoken to you are spirit and life. But some of you don't believe me." (For Jesus knew from the beginning who didn't believe, and he knew who would betray him.) Then he said, "That is what I meant when I said that people can't come to me unless the Father brings them to me."
>
> At this point many of his disciples turned away and deserted him. Then Jesus turned to the Twelve and asked, "Are you going to leave, too?"
>
> Simon Peter replied, "Lord, to whom would we go? You alone have the words that give eternal life. We believe them, and we know you are the Holy One of God."
>
> Then Jesus said, "I chose the twelve of you, but

one is a devil." He was speaking of Judas, son of Simon
Iscariot, one of the Twelve, who would betray him.
(John 6:60-71)

This last part of chapter 6 contains John's significant substitution for the confession of Peter found in the Synoptics. John provides the account of Simon's loyal despair. What brings the two
stories together is the confessional nature of both as well as the
notion of the Scandalon, the stumbling block. In the account John
substitutes, they are back at the synagogue in Capernaum, just
eighty-four feet down the street from Simon's house.

This passage represents the vital turning point in John's presentation of the ministry. Up till now it had been primarily suc-
cessful and well received. The people had only recently wanted to
make Jesus a "bread king." But Jesus understands that his mis-
placed popularity poses a significant threat to his real ministry. As
F. B. Meyer writes, "He had to undeceive them."

In the most offensive terms he can possibly come up with,
Jesus speaks the truth about what being the Passover Lamb of
God means. The focus of Passover was the eating of the Passover
lamb. Jesus has simply and graphically put two and two together
for them. This sets the scene for the scandal, failure and rejection
that will follow. This is as bad as it gets in John until the cross.

In the face of his bloody, sickening and scandalous words, many
of his disciples (John tells us) decided that enough was enough.
They could bear the burden of the scandal no longer, and so many
of them began to leave. Like the previous incident, the account
turns on a question that Jesus asks the Twelve and to which Peter
alone provides the answer. But this is a different question.

The grammar of Jesus' query indicates that the question expects the answer "No." It is sometimes translated, "You do not want to leave too, do you?" This is spoken in light of the fact that John has just informed us that many of Jesus' disciples have just deserted him.

Simon's response, spoken through slightly clenched teeth, represents an entirely different tone than the "great confession" we heard him utter at Caesarea Philippi in the Synoptic accounts. In the present context of scandal and rejection by the departing disciples, the tone here is one of loyal despair. The dilemma: Jesus is indeed a scandalous Lord—but there is no place else to go! He is the Lord; he alone possesses infinitely more than the bread he has just doled out to the hungry and confused crowd. He is the Bread of Life, the true Manna that has come down from heaven. The words that fall from his lips are alive and life-giving, no matter what scandalous effect they may have. Peter and the others he speaks for will stay to the end only because there is no place else to go. If there were another option they might have left like the others. It is only after this defining moment that Peter will begin to assert that he is willing to die with Jesus. He has begun to understand that all this may indeed end in death.

Here in the conclusion of John's substitution, it is Judas who is called a devil and not Peter, precisely because he will desert, acting on and acting out the evil influence of the evil one. Peter unwittingly spoke earlier on Satan's behalf. Judas becomes his agent knowingly and willingly.

Each one of us, if we follow him closely, that is, biblically, will come to the same moment Peter came to in John. There will be a time when you will see Jesus in a new, unexpected way, in a light you never dreamed of or wanted to see him in. He will fail to meet your expectations. You might lose a child. You might get cancer. After a lifetime of ministry you might feel rejected. You will experience him in a way that has caused countless of his other disciples to say, "This is hard; who can accept it?"

This is precisely the point where real discipleship begins. You and I have only two choices at this point. We can leave with the others. After all, it really is too much, isn't it? Or we can realize what Peter understood as he clutched on to Jesus with the last fading shred of faith he could muster. He was right, you know. There is no other place to go, no other way.

Choose, right now.

CHAPTER SEVEN

"Fear Not!"

MARK 9:2-10

Like so many other stories in the Gospels, the account usually referred to as "Jesus and the disciples on the Mount of Transfiguration" is really the story of Jesus and Peter on the mount. Though James and John are certainly there, we never hear a single word from them.

The experience was absolutely a defining moment for Simon. Jesus is transfigured. But Peter is transformed! The sight of Jesus in his true glory confirms that Peter's earlier confession was true. Jesus is the Messiah! He is the glorious Son of the living God.

> Six days later Jesus took Peter, James, and John to the top of a mountain. No one else was there. As the men watched, Jesus' appearance changed, and his clothing became dazzling white, far whiter than any earthly process could ever make it. Then Elijah and Moses appeared and began talking with Jesus.
>
> "Teacher, this is wonderful!" Peter exclaimed. "We

will make three shrines—one for you, one for Moses, and one for Elijah." He didn't really know what to say, for they were all terribly afraid.

Then a cloud came over them, and a voice from the cloud said, "This is my beloved Son. Listen to him." Suddenly they looked around, and Moses and Elijah were gone, and only Jesus was with them. As they descended the mountainside, he told them not to tell anyone what they had seen until he, the Son of Man, had risen from the dead. So they kept it to themselves, but they often asked each other what he meant by "rising from the dead." (Mark 9:2-10)

The account comes and goes in a flash, like the burst of light that was Jesus' transfigured face. This is not a transformation—that is, Jesus does not change his form. Rather, the Three are allowed to see Jesus' true nature, as he has been all along, only their eyes have just now been opened. The veil is lifted for a few precious minutes.

Six days ago Jesus had made a fantastic promise to the disciples. "I assure you that some of you standing here right now will not die before you see the Kingdom of God arrive in great power!" (Mark 9:1). Though there are other interpretations of Jesus' statement, I believe this transcendent experience on the mountain is the fulfillment of that enigmatic promise to Peter, James and John, three-fourths of the old fishing company.

The account is wrapped up in Old Testament imagery. In Exodus 24:16, six days is the time of preparation for revelation. Jesus' transfiguration will become the most powerful revelation of his glory that any of the disciples will ever see. When they witness the cross, all they will see is a man being tortured to death. The glorious resurrection will not be witnessed by anyone except two angels. This moment of transfiguration will be the only revelation of the true nature of his glory until the parousia—his coming again in clouds of glory.

If six days is the Old Testament time of preparation for revelation, then a high mountain is most certainly always the place, be it Sinai (Exodus 24) or Horeb (1 Kings 19), where (interestingly enough) both Moses and Elijah, who will shortly step onto the stage, also experienced their own glorious visions of God.

Only Luke, with his emphasis on prayer, tells us that the transfiguration was a response to Jesus' prayer (Luke 9:29). It was during his prayer that Jesus was "transfigured." His countenance as well as his clothing became as bright as light itself. Only in Mark do we find Peter's homespun description of the brightness in terms of a fuller's ability to bleach clothes. What the Three are witnessing is nothing less than unveiled glory. Peter has made his confession, has faced his moment of loyal despair, and now he experiences a vision of who Jesus really is. This is who Jesus has been all along. Now Peter sees it—and he is never the same again.

All at once ("Look!" says Luke) they see that Jesus is no longer alone. There is no explanation as to how the Three recognize the identities of Moses and Elijah; nevertheless, they are aware of the fact that they are suddenly in the presence of two of the greatest figures of the Old Testament. And so the Old Testament context comes into even sharper focus as they gaze on the faces of the two great prophets. Only Luke tells us what they were discussing with Jesus. He uses the word *exodus*. They were talking about Jesus' upcoming exodus at Jerusalem.

Both of these legendary men have come up in the context of

Jesus' ministry. We read earlier that some people had confused Jesus with "the Elijah who was to come." But here are the two of them together, so that clearly cannot be what is happening. Also, especially in John's Gospel, the primary Old Testament image for communicating who Jesus is and what his ministry is all about is Deuteronomy 18 and the "prophet like Moses." This person would do as Moses did. He would communicate to the people only what God had told him to say. Again and again in John, Jesus insists he is only speaking God's word. More than once the crowd will speculate whether Jesus is "the Prophet" (John 6:14; 7:40). But these are not images. They are living, breathing men. And Peter has the privilege of listening in on their conversation with Jesus.

From this point on, the prospect of Jesus' exodus, or leaving, will represent a dark foreboding for Peter. Elijah, "the restorer of all things" (Mark 9:12), is present. Moses, the one who pleaded to see the face and the glory of God, is finally receiving the answer to his request, all these centuries later. Paul speaks of "the knowledge of the glory of God in the face of Christ" (2 Corinthians 4:6 NASB). That knowledge, that Truth, is now blazing before Peter, James and John.

He Did Not Know What He Was Saying

As always, it is only Peter who speaks up. Mark tells us, "He did not know what to say" (Mark 9:6 NIV). He didn't really know what to say, for they were all terribly afraid.

This almost certainly indicates that what he did say he should not have said. We are told that the reason he did not know what to say was that he was terrified. Luke lets us know that the reason he spoke was that the "men" seemed to be leaving. Certainly the situation called for some sort of response! But the appropriate one was beyond Simon.

What he does say has puzzled scholars from the beginning. Should it be "It is good that we are here" or "Is it good for us to be here?" Common sense appeals to the second translation. It best fits the fact that he was terrified.

Then comes that most curious offer to build three "tents," one for Jesus and two more for Moses and Elijah.

The traditional interpretation takes the word for "tent" to refer to the booths that were set up to commemorate the Festival of Tabernacles (also known as Feast of Booths or *Sukkoth*). Seen in this light, Peter is inviting them to stay a little longer and celebrate the feast together. After all, Zechariah 14:16-19 speaks of booths as being a part of the celebration of the final kingdom. Perhaps Peter believes this really is the final moment, the coming of the kingdom of God. Were you and I to witness what he saw, perhaps we might believe the same thing.

But this is more a Sinai story, is it not? There's the high mountain and the glory and the cloud. A newer and, it seems to me, more likely interpretation is that the tents Peter proposes building are more in line with the tabernacle. The Greek word he uses is also used in the Septuagint to describe the tabernacle of Moses. Isn't Moses standing there, after all? Is he not, once again, meeting with God? And didn't Moses himself experience a sort of transfiguration at Sinai? (See Exodus 34:29-35.)

If all this is true, then what Peter has in mind is not extending their time together in some sort of religious holiday. He is trying, though incorrectly, to deal with his terror. He knows that no one could see the unveiled glory of God and live. His terror is based on a genuine fear for his own life and those of his two friends. Has he not once before begged Jesus to go away from him when he became fearfully aware of his sinfulness before the power of Jesus? In this interpretation the tents are meant to veil the radiance of the three holy figures in order to protect Peter and his companions. What happens next would seem to confirm Peter's fear. God provides a cloud to envelop and afford the disciples the protection they want but no longer need.

During their earthly ministries, both Moses and Elijah had encountered this cloud. Both of them had heard the voice of God (Deuteronomy 18:15; 1 Kings 17:2). Matthew tells us that the disciples fell face down, terrified, when they heard the Voice. Luke says they were terrified as they entered the cloud. The cloud is said to have "overshadowed" them. This is the same word that was used of the Spirit of God "overshadowing" Mary at the moment of the incarnation. Perhaps now the potential for a new understanding can be born in the hearts of the disciples. The voice Jesus heard at his baptism, at the inauguration of his ministry, is heard once more as he nears its completion, as he makes ready for his "exodus."

Having fallen to the ground in terror a moment before, the disciples look up and see only Jesus. He is himself once more, ordinary. He walks over to Peter and touches him on the shoulder. "Don't be afraid," he says with a peculiar look on his face that Peter has never seen there before. Whenever he is revealed to them, those are always the first words on his lips. When the nets were miraculously filled, he looked down at the kneeling Peter and said, "Don't be afraid; from now on you'll catch men." When he calmed the demonic storm on the sea he asked, "Why were you afraid?" As he approached their boat, walking on the water, he called out, "I am, don't be afraid;" And now as the terror is draining from their faces he speaks those same comforting words. When later he is raised from the dead, he will speak them to the women at the tomb: "Don't be afraid." What Brennan Manning says is true: "If you don't have to be afraid of God, you don't have to be afraid of anything."

Mark tells us that as they were making their way back down the mountain the disciples discussed what Jesus meant when he spoke of "rising from the dead." The question will plague Peter even after the resurrection when, after seeing the empty tomb, he will still wonder to himself what had happened (Luke 24:12). Revelation and terror—how often in our experience have they been linked? Have you ever experienced the terrifying splendor of Jesus?

On that mount Peter and the others got a glimpse into heaven. He discovered that not all mysteries will be explained there, but instead we will know how truly vast and unknowable the mystery of Christ is. Of all that he might have recounted, this incident on the mount is the only historical experience with Jesus to which Peter refers in his letters!

> And he received honor and glory from God the Father when God's glorious, majestic voice called down from heaven, "This is my beloved Son; I am fully pleased with him." We ourselves heard the voice when we were there with him on the holy mountain. (2 Peter 1:17-18)

CHAPTER EIGHT

Back to Fishing

MATTHEW 17:24-27

Simon's familiar hometown, Capernaum, seemed to have changed as he and Jesus made their way back to his house, their base of operations in Galilee. Peter was still trying to cope with what Jesus had just revealed to them—that he was soon to die. Jesus' promise of resurrection might have provided a measure of comfort to Peter, if only he or any of the others had been able to grasp it. The last few days had been a roller-coaster ride for them all. First there was the intensity of his confession, then the dazzling transfiguration of Jesus on the mountaintop. How is a pious Jewish man supposed to recover after seeing Moses and Elijah?

As they made their way down the narrow alley, past the synagogue to his home, Peter remembered the last time they were here together. He remembered the excited crowd pressing into the courtyard just to catch a glimpse of Jesus. He remembered as well those fanatics who tore a hole in the roof to lower their paralyzed friend down through. His wife still rolled her eyes whenever that section of the roof leaked.

But now the crowds were gone. What's more, the excitement was missing too. They were, all of them, bone tired from their long journey. They were emotionally exhausted as well from dealing with all that Jesus had said about what awaited him in Jerusalem in the weeks to come. As far as we know, it was to be their last time in Capernaum together.

> On their arrival in Capernaum, the tax collectors for the Temple tax came to Peter and asked him, "Doesn't your teacher pay the Temple tax?"
>
> "Of course he does," Peter replied. Then he went into the house to talk to Jesus about it.
>
> But before he had a chance to speak, Jesus asked him, "What do you think, Peter? Do kings tax their own people or the foreigners they have conquered?"
>
> "They tax the foreigners," Peter replied.
>
> "Well, then," Jesus said, "the citizens are free! However, we don't want to offend them, so go down to the lake and throw in a line. Open the mouth of the first fish you catch, and you will find a coin. Take the coin and pay the tax for both of us." (Matthew 17:24-27)

It seems natural that Matthew, the ex-tax collector, would be the only Gospel writer to record this story. These were not the same sort of tax collectors as he had been. Matthew had treacherously represented the hated Romans and extorted taxes from his own people. These were men from the synagogue, and this tax was a Jewish one. It was based on Exodus 30:15: "When this offering is given to the LORD to make atonement for yourselves, the rich must not give more, and the poor must not give less. Use this money for the care of the Tabernacle."

As far as Peter could remember, Jesus had never been asked to pay this tax before. This was, after all, a voluntary tax, which is why it was open to question in the first place. It was the commonly accepted custom of the day that religious teachers were exempted from this particular tax. This was not a Roman tax. If it were, would there be any question about paying it or not? After A.D. 70 and the destruction of Jerusalem, the Romans appropriated this tax to support the new Roman temple to Jupiter Capitalinus.

The very fact that the temple tax collectors had come to ask at all was still another indication that much had changed in Capernaum—that Jesus' reputation was beginning to erode. It must have seemed too great an emotional leap for the tired fisherman to return from his mountaintop vision to the drudgery of taxes.

Their question is grammatically constructed to expect an affirmative answer: "He does pay the tax, doesn't he?" At the heart of the issue may be Jesus' loyalty to the temple. Will he allow himself to be further seen as being somehow anti-temple? After all, his first public action was to tear up the temple market, the Bazaar of Annas. It was still an open question.

Peter automatically, as if conditioned by a lifetime of submitting to synagogue authority, answers, "Yes, of course he does." As soon as the words left his lips he feels that it was the wrong answer.

The Answer Before the Question

As Peter stepped inside the house, it was Jesus who was the first to speak. "What do you think, Simon?" he said with tiredness in his voice that matched Peter's. Peter could not remember Jesus ever asking him what he thought in this way. "Who pays taxes, sons or aliens?"

Is this about those synagogue people at the gate? Peter asked himself. It seemed a fair enough question.

"Why, aliens, of course," he hesitantly answered.

"So the sons are exempt?"

"Yes, but . . ." was all he was given room to say.

"Go take your hand line and cast into the lake. The first fish you bring up will have a coin in its mouth. Use it to pay the tax for both of us. After all, we don't want to offend them."

Peter reached behind the door and took his line and hook from the peg where he always left them hanging. Without a word he wandered toward the shoreline, puzzled that after being called to be a fisher of men he was now being asked to fish for fish once more. *Since when does he* not *want to offend anyone!* he muttered as he trudged down to the shore.

We can only assume that everything happened just as Jesus said it would. Incredibly, Matthew leaves out the fulfillment of the miracle. But perhaps the miracle was not the point.

It is an enigmatic story to say the least. The depressed tone of it can be clearly read between the lines. Things had indeed changed for Jesus and his disciples in Capernaum. He was now being treated in many ways like a foreigner, being asked to pay a tax from which he was clearly exempt. His statement about not wanting to offend any-one I find to be the most miraculous and mysterious part of the story.

The commentaries often quote Matthew 22:21, "render unto Caesar," as though that statement will explain it all. But this was not Caesar's tax; it was, in effect, God's. And had not Peter only recently plainly confessed Jesus to be God's Son? There seems to me to be every reason not to pay the tax and to deliberately cause offense. But mysteriously, Jesus chooses not to do so. He elects not to exercise his and Peter's right as children of God.

Does not Paul present the idea that though we are free we should sometimes voluntarily submit to authority (Romans 14:13-23; 1 Corinthians 8:13—9:1, 12)? Though this is all true, for me it still does not explain everything away.

Maybe Jesus simply needed the heat to be off for a few days to recover and prepare for the final trip to Jerusalem and his Passion. Perhaps he was only choosing his battles. Why get caught up in something so petty when infinitely larger struggles are about to present themselves?

For the purpose of our study, the point, I believe, is the closeness that is clearly evident between Jesus and Peter. Jesus has returned to Peter's home in Capernaum, which Peter is still apparently maintaining. The tax collectors have come to Peter because obviously everyone knows that if you want to speak to Jesus, Peter, his best friend, is the man you should talk to.

And finally, Jesus' response and provision of the unseen miracle is for both their benefits. "Pay the tax for you and me," he said.

Years later, in Peter's letters, we can detect faint echoes of this peculiar incident:

> For the Lord's sake, accept all authority—the king as head of state, and the officials he has appointed. . . .
>
> It is God's will that your good lives should silence those who make foolish accusations against you. (1 Peter 2:13-15)

He is especially hard on those who follow their own evil, lustful desires and who despise authority. (2 Peter 2:10)

These are good lessons and true. We note, though, that in addition to leaving out the miracle, Matthew chose for some unknown reason to leave out the real reason for the strange story of the coin in the fish's mouth.

Once upon a time two tired servants of God stumbled back home to find no longer the faithful but instead demanding religious people waiting for them at the door. Knowing that the least indiscretion would mean more conflict for both of them, one chose to exercise his awesome and unlimited power to make appear out of nowhere a couple of dollars to pay the fee the men at the door were hounding them for. All this for the glorious purpose that the two of them might share an uninterrupted evening together of talk and meal fellowship, since in a few days they would be leaving that place, never to return.

CHAPTER NINE

Confusion at the Final Meal

JOHN 13:6-10

I t was the beginning of an extraordinary day. Jesus sent Peter and John to make the extensive preparations for the Passover meal (Luke 22:7). Because Jesus and his disciples were Galileans, they celebrated the Passover in the tradition of the Diaspora community.

When the Jews were dispersed (hence the term *Diaspora*) after the fall of the Northern Kingdom in 721 B.C., the scattered community made it a practice to celebrate the great festivals a day early, just in case the calendar had been accidentally miscalculated. This explains why Jesus and his disciples were celebrating their Passover on Thursday while everyone else in Jerusalem was making preparations on Friday. This means the Jews of Jerusalem were selecting and slaughtering their Passover lambs at precisely the same moment the following day, when Jesus, the Lamb of God, was dying on the cross.

Peter and John were sent to purchase bitter herbs, parsley, wine and *charoset*, a mixture of ground apples, raisins, almonds and cinnamon that symbolized the mortar their ancestors were forced to mix in Egypt. Most important, they would have chosen a lamb and had it certified as "spotless" by a priest at the temple. Did either of them see any connection between the innocent creature they purchased that morning and the one who awaited them when they returned from their errands? They would also be responsible for arranging the furnishings in the upper room, which Jesus had said were already there.

Up to this point, as we have seen, a good case can be made for Peter's being the leader of the Twelve. How did he react when given this menial chore? Luke tells us that during their final journey to Jerusalem, more than once the disciples had argued about who among them was the greatest. I can't help but believe that Jesus gave Peter this menial task to help prepare him for the lesson he would receive that night at the table. Jesus deliberately cast Peter and John in the role of servants.

Matthew tells us that Jesus began the meal by predicting that one of them would betray him (26:21). What would have been the effect of this kind of statement on the tone of the rest of the evening?

We can reconstruct the seating arrangement around Jesus that evening. John is close enough to lean against Jesus and whisper in his ear. Jesus would have been reclining, leaning on his left elbow. This means John is probably on his right (John 13:23). In Judaism, as in many other ancient cultures, the right hand is the place of honor. Judas, it seems, is sitting at his left. This was called

A FRAGILE STONE

"the place of the intimate friend." Jesus can dip the sop in the same dish with him (Mark 14:20). Judas is also close enough that Jesus is able to confirm his treachery privately (Matthew 26:25). Had the other disciples heard that Judas was the one, he would have never left the room alive. Could it be that Judas had been given Peter's usual place for the meal?

One person we cannot place is Peter. He is able only to motion to John, "Ask him which one he means" (John 13:24). Perhaps he is moving around the table, serving the various elements of the meal, since he has helped make all the preparations with John. But there's John, sitting in the place of honor. Surely we can only speculate how Simon might have felt about all this. Luke tells us that at the end of the meal an argument broke out among them as to who was the greatest (Luke 22:24). Again, it is only speculation, but who was most likely to have been in the mood to argue about their position?

John tells us that at some point late in the meal (and certainly in response to their argument), Jesus silently rose from his place and made his way over to the large stone water jars that had been provided for the ceremonial washing of hands before the meal. They had talked about this issue of who was the greatest again and again. He had told them more than one parable about it on their final journey to Jerusalem. But now Jesus gives up on words and enacts a living parable for the Twelve. He gets up from the table, takes off his coat, very deliberately wraps a towel around his waist and fills a basin with water. By this point they must have been silently wondering what was going on, not able to guess until the last moment what he was up to.

If you look closely at the story usually referred to as "the washing of the disciples' feet," you'll see that it is actually the story of the washing of Peter's feet. He and Jesus are the only two characters on the stage at this point. Jesus' demeanor betrays no bitterness toward the ones who will shortly betray him; there is in him no sense of approaching danger. He slowly makes his way around the triclinium, or three-sided table. He is dressed like a slave. He is acting like a slave.

During the flowering of the rabbinic period, some of the rabbis became concerned that their disciples were becoming overzealous in regard to their rabbinic masters. They felt that some limits needed to be put into place. One of those limits read, "Every task that the slave does for his master will the disciple do for his teacher except one. He shall not loose the thong of his sandal" (b. Ketuboth 96a). This mandate must have been on John the Baptist's mind when he said of Jesus, "I am not worthy to loosen the thong of his sandal." This was surely a genuine demonstration of John's humility. But how much greater is the humility of the Teacher who is willing to reverse things and serve his disciples— not only loosening their sandals but also washing their feet! The washing of Peter's feet is meant to be a lesson in humility and servanthood, a lesson that he perhaps was supposed to start learning that very morning.

> When he came to Simon Peter, Peter said to him, "Lord, why are you going to wash my feet?"
>
> Jesus replied, "You don't understand now why I am doing it; someday you will."
>
> "No," Peter protested, "you will never wash my feet!"

Jesus replied, "But if I don't wash you, you won't belong to me."

Simon Peter exclaimed, "Then wash my hands and head as well, Lord, not just my feet!"

Jesus replied, "A person who has bathed all over does not need to wash, except for the feet, to be entirely clean. And you are clean, but that isn't true of everyone here." For Jesus knew who would betray him. That is what he meant when he said, "Not all of you are clean." (John 13:6-11)

An Appropriate Refusal

Peter's first statement in verse 6 is emphatic in the Greek: "You . . . my feet . . . wash!" It is the end of a difficult day for Simon, and his tone betrays his nervousness. Little does he know that the day has only begun.

Peter was right! It was inappropriate for Jesus to be doing what he was doing. In Simon's and everyone else's mind the Messiah would never suffer, never submit, never serve. By the end of this long day Jesus will have done all three. And Simon will be bitterly disappointed with him. Jesus will fail to meet his expectations as the Christ—perhaps even, that evening, as his friend. The world Peter had built around Jesus has begun to slowly fall apart. He has fallen victim to one of the great paradoxes of life as described by Kierkegaard: "Life must be lived forward but it can only be understood backwards."

Jesus' first reply, "You do not realize now what I am doing, but later you will understand," sounds calm and controlled. After all, Jesus is the Servant/Lord. It has been the consistent shape of his life from their very first meeting. When they were tired he would make sure they got away to a quiet place for some rest (Mark 6:31). When they were hungry he fed them, even after his resurrection (John 21:12-13).

"No," said Peter, "you shall never wash my feet." Perhaps his tone is surly here, taking into account his difficult and disappointing day. Simon, we recall again, is the only one of the disciples who ever says "no" to Jesus. At this moment it is not a rejection of Jesus' friendship. It is a denial of who he really is: their Servant Lord. In essence, Peter is trying to say to Jesus, "You just don't get it, do you? This is not appropriate. Of all the inappropriate things that you've done, this is the most inappropriate."

John the Baptist alluded to the same dilemma when Jesus asked to be baptized by him. "This is not appropriate. You should be baptizing me." He embraces sinners, and the Pharisees say, "What you're doing is not appropriate." He reaches out to prostitutes, he touches lepers, he touches the dead, and everyone says, "This is not appropriate."

In order to enter into the emotional dimension of the story, we must first see how right in his own eyes Peter was to protest! Jesus is asking him to submit in humility to his servant lordship. Of all that he had been asked to do in the previous three years, this is the most difficult for Simon. Remember, Peter had only recently seen Jesus transfigured on Tabor. The radiant and intimate companion of Moses and Elijah kneeling before him and washing his feet? Never!

Jesus' tone becomes more severe. "Unless I wash you, you have no part with me." Peter's denial is serious business. Jesus hinges his salvation, his discipleship on it. But for Peter in his confusion, this no doubt feels like more rejection. Jesus' point is that if Peter denies the humility of his Servant Savior, he cannot possibly take part in what Jesus is doing. His refusal to be served by Jesus renders him unusable as a future servant of Jesus. Until Peter submits to who Jesus really is, how can he become one of his disciples? For that matter, how can we?

Too often Peter's character is drawn in only one dimension. Too often the complex tangle of his emotional life is oversimplified. But here clearly his passion causes him to go overboard. "Then wash my hands and head as well, Lord, not just my feet!" Though he clearly did so a moment ago, he does not mean to say "no" to Jesus. If he could take back those vehement words, he would do so now.

Jesus' peaceful demeanor has returned. He is once more the Teacher. "A person who has bathed all over does not need to wash, except for the feet, to be entirely clean. And you are clean, but that isn't true of everyone here."

Judas had gone to the high priest six days earlier with the question, "How much will you pay me to betray Jesus to you?" (Matthew 26:15). Though he sits there with freshly washed feet, Judas is definitely not clean.

Luke tells us that after the dispute about who was the greatest (and presumably after John's account of the footwashing), Jesus sums up the lesson in humility: "But among you, those who are the greatest should take the lowest rank, and the leader should be like a servant. Normally the master sits at the table and is served by his servants. But not here! For I am your servant" (Luke 22:26-27).

Next he turns to Simon, the one for whom, above all the others, the lesson was meant.

> "Simon, Simon, Satan has asked to have all of you, to sift you like wheat. But I have pleaded in prayer for you, Simon, that your faith should not fail. So when you have repented and turned to me again, strengthen and build up your brothers."
>
> Peter said, "Lord, I am ready to go to prison with you, and even to die with you."
>
> But Jesus said, "Peter, let me tell you something. The rooster will not crow tomorrow morning until you have denied three times that you even know me." (Luke 22:31-34)

Sifted Like Wheat

Like some New Testament parallel to the book of Job, Satan has come before the throne of God asking to inflict his worst on Simon, and some sort of holy arrangement has been made. They will all be sifted. But it is Simon Peter for whom Jesus specifically prays. In Jesus' mind that was how it was supposed to happen. All of them will go through the torture of seeing Jesus die on the cross. But Simon will be the one whose faith will ultimately not fail, all because of the prayers of his best friend, Jesus. He will repent, turn around and become a source of strength to his brothers. In fact, the fragile stone, strengthened by the prayers of Christ, will become a source of strength for his brothers and sisters of all the centuries ahead. It is Jesus' prayers that make Simon strong.

Peter does not hear the second part of Jesus' pronouncement, the part about his being prayed for and being restored. He has become suspicious at last that this is somehow all about prison and even death. He means literally what he says when he pledges his life to Jesus. Remember, in just a few hours, he will be the only one to draw his sword and fling himself in the midst of at least two hundred armed soldiers in the garden.

Finally comes the last and most disheartening word from Jesus. Peter, he predicts, will deny him three times. It is the final punch in his solar plexus. Throughout the evening Simon has faltered again and again, but always he has tried to come back, to reconnect somehow with Jesus. After this blow he will remain curiously silent for the rest of the evening.

The meal finished, they vacantly sing a hymn and leave for the garden. They are, all of them, confused, sorrowful and supremely disillusioned. But none of them more than Simon, son of Jonah.

CHAPTER TEN

Dismay in the Garden

MARK 14:27-42

M atthew tells us that on their way to the garden, after the Last Supper, Jesus once again made a prediction that his disciples would fail to stand by him.

"All of you will desert me," Jesus told them. "For the Scriptures say,

'I will strike the Shepherd,
and the sheep will be scattered.'

But after I am raised from the dead, I will go ahead of you to Galilee and meet you there."

Peter said to him, "Even if everyone else deserts you, I never will."

"Peter," Jesus replied, "the truth is, this very night, before the rooster crows twice, you will deny me three times."

"No!" Peter insisted. "Not even if I have to die with you! I will never deny you!" And all the others vowed the same. (Mark 14:27-31)

It is impossible to divine the state of Peter's heart and mind just now. For certain he is confused and discouraged. Jesus' predictions of their failing have become more narrowly focused on Peter. It is unfair to assume that the tone of Peter's assertions in verses 33 and 35 are boastful. He is bewildered by the cumulative weight of Jesus' statements. What he affirms he believes in his heart to be true.

The Eleven arrived together at the estate called Gethsemane. This was a resting place that Jesus frequented. It may have been owned by one of his wealthier followers, perhaps the same man who loaned them the upper room for their Passover. The setting, in the grove of olive trees, away from the crush of the city, provided the kind of peaceful surroundings Jesus favored. In A.D. 70, Titus would strip the flanks of the Mount of Olives during the siege of Jerusalem, using most of the wood for crosses. But the garden Peter rested in now was lined with terraces of olive trees.

> And they came to an olive grove called Gethsemane, and Jesus said, "Sit here while I go and pray." He took Peter, James, and John with him, and he began to be filled with horror and deep distress. He told them, "My soul is crushed with grief to the point of death. Stay here and watch with me."
>
> He went on a little farther and fell face down on the ground. He prayed that, if it were possible, the awful hour awaiting him might pass him by. "Abba, Father," he said, "everything is possible for you. Please take this cup of suffering away from me. Yet I want your will, not mine."
>
> Then he returned and found the disciples asleep. "Simon!" he said to Peter. "Are you asleep? Couldn't you stay awake and watch with me even one hour? Keep

alert and pray. Otherwise temptation will overpower you. For though the spirit is willing enough, the body is weak."

Then Jesus left them again and prayed, repeating his pleadings. Again he returned to them and found them sleeping, for they just couldn't keep their eyes open. And they didn't know what to say.

When he returned to them the third time, he said, "Still sleeping? Still resting? Enough! The time has come. I, the Son of Man, am betrayed into the hands of sinners. Up, let's be going. See, my betrayer is here!" (Mark 14:32-42)

Jesus leaves eight of his disciples at the entrance to the garden with no other instructions but "Sit here." He then takes the Three further into the garden and into his confidence. They have not been asked along simply because of Jesus' need for companionship during this dark time. They are asked to stay close in order to keep a watch. The soldiers will be coming shortly. (When they do arrive, it will be Jesus who first detects their coming, not the three incompetent lookouts.) Jesus confides, as he walks further into the moonlit grove, that the grief he has begun to struggle with is about to crush the life out of him. His will is about to come into mortal conflict with the will of the Father, and it is breaking his heart. We hear no response whatsoever from the confused disciples to Jesus' painful confession. Hearing Jesus talk like this only makes them more afraid.

He walks a few steps and gives way to the passionate grief that is bearing down upon him. Peter remembers that he literally fell on his face under the weight of it, the way he would soon fall under the weight of the crossbeam. He cries out like a little boy,

"Abba—everything is possible for you." And indeed everything is possible for his Father. If Jesus had ultimately refused the cup, the Father would have taken it away. And in that moment we would all have been lost. Yet the Son is able to choke out the words "I want your will not mine," confessing that for this moment he does not want the cup he is being offered—but if it is the Father's will, he will drink it to the dregs. If James and John were still awake at this point, I wonder if they understood the reference to the cup they themselves had said they were ready to drink (Mark 10:38-40). Genuine obedience is not doing something we already want to do, but submitting to the last thing in the world we would do. The prayerful obedience of Jesus in the garden made possible the cross. Prayer makes everything possible.

Jesus picks himself up from the wet ground and staggers back to the Three, miraculously to check on them, and finds that they have given way to sleep. In the military this would be an offense punishable by death—being asleep at your post.

Though all three are soundly asleep, it is only Simon whom Jesus castigates. You can hear the tired disappointment in his voice: "Simon, couldn't you stay awake?" Earlier Peter had sworn he would follow Jesus to prison and even to death. Now he could not find it in himself to stay awake to watch with his agonizing Friend. Jesus, however, in the midst of his suffering, returns to make sure they are not falling into temptation. He had been praying for Peter. Now he instructs Peter to pray for himself. The story of the Garden of Gethsemane is a story of the importance of prayer. Without the prayers of Jesus we would not know his salvation. When Jesus says that the spirit is willing but the flesh is weak, I wonder if he was referring to both his own and the disciples' struggles.

There are no details about the contents of his third season of prayer. Perhaps there were no words that Peter could remember, only sighs and unutterable groanings. Only Luke tells us that an angel appeared during this final painful period, to strengthen Jesus. It is only after the angel comes that the intensity of his prayer rises to the point that his sweat becomes like drops of blood, a detail only Luke the doctor records (Luke 22:44).

When he returns for the third and final time, they are once more asleep. Luke says "exhausted from sorrow." Peter's response on being awakened for the third time? Mark records that he did not know what to say. Jesus too is exhausted from grief and sorrow—and, no doubt, bitter disappointment.

Courage in the Face of the Cohort

The time for prayer has come to an end. The Three have failed him yet again, and Judas and his cohort are at the gate. There has been no alarm from the eight who were left outside, and so we can only assume they have fallen asleep as well or else fled.

The scattering rays of torchlight through the olive trees must have confused the sleepy disciples. What was it like for them to awaken with a jolt at the clamoring of at least two hundred men encircling them in the pale light of the full Passover moon? We hear not a peep from any of them. Only one has the courage to act.

> Jesus fully realized all that was going to happen to him. Stepping forward to meet them, he asked, "Whom are you looking for?"

"Jesus of Nazareth," they replied.

"I am he," Jesus said. Judas was standing there with them when Jesus identified himself. And as he said, "I am he," they all fell backward to the ground! Once more he asked them, "Whom are you searching for?"

And again they replied, "Jesus of Nazareth."

"I told you that I am he," Jesus said. "And since I am the one you want, let these others go." He did this to fulfill his own statement: "I have not lost a single one of those you gave me."

Then Simon Peter drew a sword and slashed off the right ear of Malchus, the high priest's servant. But Jesus said to Peter, "Put your sword back into its sheath. Shall I not drink from the cup the Father has given me?" (John 18:4-11)

As the armed men approach, a curious incident occurs. Jesus bravely goes out to meet them. The fact that they have torches and lanterns indicates they were expecting a search, certainly not expecting that the person they were looking for would be the first to confront them.

"I am," Jesus responds. Both groups, the Roman soldiers as well as the contingent of Jewish priests and temple guards, fall to the ground—for two completely different reasons. The Jews have heard someone speak the unspeakable Name. They fall down in fear. Why do the Roman legionnaires back up and fall to the ground? Do they expect an ambush? Or perhaps they are simply awed at seeing Jesus' command of the situation.

"Take me and let these men go." Jesus strangely is in charge of the soldiers. John records that this fulfilled one of Jesus' earlier prayer requests. His prayers were already taking effect.

Earlier, Luke records, Jesus had had a discussion with the disciples about their purchasing swords (22:36). Now it seems to one of them that the time for swords has come. All of the Gospels record Peter's attack on Malchus. Strangely, none of the Synoptics mention his name; only John does. Maybe Matthew, Mark and Luke wanted to keep his identity under wraps, since they were writing to primarily Roman readers and it wouldn't do to put any additional heat on their brother Peter, who was by that time a pillar in the church at Rome. Though it was the wrong thing to do, at least Peter did something! The fact that he would attack in the face of what seemed to be such hopeless odds tells us much about the courage of his character. Remember that the disciples had with them at least two swords that night in the garden. Only one was drawn. In the scenes to come, especially the one in the courtyard at Caiaphas's house, we will see that he was motivated not by fear but something far more powerful. I sincerely believe that there was not a cowardly bone in his body.

A Bleeding Ear

Luke gives us the forensic details we need to reconstruct Peter's attack. If we had only Matthew and Mark we would have to assume a vertical stroke that took off Malchus's ear. Luke, with his love for medical detail, tells us that what Peter sliced off was the servant's earlobe, or "little ear." This would call for a swiping, horizontal stroke. We can picture then Peter rushing forward, brandishing his short sword from under his cloak, and aiming for the throat of the closest person. At the last moment Malchus falls back, turning his head, and loses only his earlobe, which Jesus is able to heal in the confusion apparently without anyone taking notice. If it had been seen that Peter had caused bloodshed, he would doubtless have been arrested as well.

What a day! Peter had not expected to be called upon as a servant to prepare the meal. He had not expected to find Judas sitting at his place beside Jesus at the meal. He had certainly not expected to see the Master, who only a few days earlier had been resplendent in light, kneeling before him like a common slave, washing his dirty feet. He had not expected to see the emotional breakdown he had just witnessed in the garden. Never in his wildest imagination had he expected Jesus, in a desperate moment like this, to correct him like a schoolboy. Peter had been rebuked for what he would have thought was the very proof of his faithfulness to Jesus. After all, shouldn't his courage in the garden be something a person called the Rock should possess? But above all, never had he expected to see Jesus give up.

Peter could bear all the rest of it, but not this. Peter gives up his fight only because he thinks he sees Jesus giving up. Jesus, it seemed, was turning his back on all he had so passionately preached about for the last three years. *What about the kingdom?* Peter screamed inside himself. Seeing Jesus submit to being bound and led away broke something deep in Peter's will.

We must understand that this was the culmination in a long series of confusing disappointments that evening for Peter. Jesus had profoundly failed to meet Peter's expectations, not because there was anything wrong with Jesus but because, even after three years together, Peter still failed to understand what Jesus meant when he called himself the Messiah. Jesus' greatest disappointment to Peter would occur in just two more days, when he would die on the cross like a slave, like a criminal. You and I will never fully understand that moment until we feel the depth of the disappointment in Peter's heart and soul as he stood before that cross. At that moment nothing seemed more certain than that it had all been a lie.

Years later, as an old man, Peter, who calls himself "the Elder," will echo the lessons he learned on this very night. His first letter, which is a treaty on suffering, shows that he finally came to understand that the call is not to evade or destroy the source of the suffering but, like Jesus did that night, to embrace it with all the courage God makes available through faith. In Acts we will see Peter living out this very lesson. And the sting of being found asleep three times at his post he echoes three times in his letters:

Prepare your minds for action. (1 Peter 1:13 NIV)

Be self controlled and alert. (1 Peter 5:8 NIV)

Be on your guard. (2 Peter 3:17 NIV)

CHAPTER ELEVEN

The Despairing Denier

MARK 14:66-72

T he past several hours had been a nightmare for Simon. He longed to wake up to his old, familiar and safe world. But it no longer existed.

Of all the confusion storming through his poor mind that night, one tormenting thought must have seemed most certain above all the others: he would never see Jesus again. Everything he believed Jesus to be had vanished like a mist in the course of the evening. In the back of his mind he had been hoping, like the others, for a throne in Jerusalem. The transfiguration had affirmed it all completely. Had that been a hallucination? Certainly the last three years had not been. He had seen every conceivable prophecy vividly fulfilled in detail. Peter's concept of Messiah could be summed up this way: "The Messiah will never submit, surrender or serve." And yet Jesus had done all three in a matter of a few hours!

Peter and John followed close behind the mob, always keeping

Jesus in view. As they made their way toward Caiaphas's house, Peter felt the agony of separation. Since that first morning together by the lake he had rarely left Jesus' side. Even now, he was keeping as close as possible. It is impossible to delve into the emotional turbulence he was negotiating. When faced with Jesus' prophecies of his denials he had declared, "Even if everyone else deserts you, I never will!" (Mark 14:29). What kind of person makes these kinds of statements?

"I am ready to die for you," he had insisted (John 13:37). "Even if everyone else deserts you, I never will"(Matthew 26:33). "Not even if I have to die with you! I will never deny you" (Matthew 26:35). Jesus had given Peter an important role as the leader of the Twelve. In his confusion and insecurity, Peter had tried to grab that authority for himself. After this night he would never grasp his position so tightly again. In fact, we will see that he will eventually let it go.

> Meanwhile, Peter was below in the courtyard. One of the servant girls who worked for the high priest noticed Peter warming himself at the fire. She looked at him closely and then said, "You also were one of those with Jesus, the Nazarene."
>
> Peter denied it. "I don't know what you're talking about," he said, and he went out into the entryway. Just then, a rooster crowed.
>
> The servant girl saw him standing there and began telling the others, "That man is definitely one of them!" Peter denied it again.
>
> A little later some other bystanders began saying to Peter, "You must be one of them because you are from Galilee."
>
> Peter said, "I swear by God, I don't know this man

you're talking about." And immediately the rooster crowed the second time. Suddenly, Jesus' words flashed through Peter's mind: "Before the rooster crows twice, you will deny me three times." And he broke down and cried. (Mark 14:66-72)

All four Gospels tell the story of Peter's denial. It was an important message for the early church, faced as they were with the same temptation to deny Jesus before their Roman persecutors. It is also the vital key to understanding the rest of Peter's life. The heartbreaking denials provide an emotional window into the heart of the man he would become. It broke Peter in the best sense of the word.

Each Evangelist accounts for the three denials—two initial queries followed an hour later by a third, more direct confrontation that causes Peter not to curse but to swear an oath, something Jesus had urged them never to do (Matthew 5:37).

Look carefully at the wording of the first two questions from the Synoptics, "You *also* were with him . . ." (see Matthew 26:69; Mark 14:67; Luke 22:58 NIV). This word *also* points to a detail fleshed out for us only in John. John tells us that he also accompanied Peter to Caiaphas's house, and because he was known to the girl at the door, he was able to go straight into the courtyard. Tradition says that John knew her because he had once delivered fish there when he was still working with his father, Zebedee. A fish market has been excavated in Jerusalem that has been designated as belonging to Zebedee. Note that John also knows the high priest's servant's name, Malchus. He alone knows even that the man who asked the final question of Peter was a relative of Malchus.

What is important for us to realize, however, is not John's inside knowledge of people and places. What matters most is the *also*. It tells us that John was there as an acknowledged follower of Jesus. When the girl sees Peter warming himself by the fire and later standing alone at the gate, she assumes he is *another* of Jesus' disciples. A different tone is set once we know that John was there as well and that he had to first leave Peter waiting at the door and then, in effect, get permission for him to enter. Peter is not skulking in the shadows. He is there in association with another known follower of Jesus, namely John. It seems all the other disciples have fled except these two. On resurrection morning they alone will have the courage to venture out to check on the empty tomb.

The third and final question is in fact two questions at once. About an hour later someone other than the girl notices Peter's thick Galilean accent. The Talmud speaks of the distinctive drawl of those from Galilee (*Megillah*, 24b). At last, John tells us of the final straw. "A relative of the man whose ear Peter had cut off challenged him, 'Didn't I see you with him in the olive grove?'" (John 18:26 NIV).

Peter had been in possession of an illegal sword. What's more, he had used it against this man's relative, attempting to cut his throat, though it is difficult to determine if anyone saw the wounding or the healing of Malchus's ear in all the confusion. We are meant to feel the cumulative weight of the three questions, especially in the Gospel of John, where, to heighten the tension, John inserts a section on Jesus' questioning before Caiaphas before he presents the final denial of Peter. Could it be that at that moment Peter remembered Jesus' word in Luke, "If anyone denies me here on earth, I will deny that person before God's angels" (Luke 12:9)? But surely that is not what finally broke him.

Along with the pressure of being identified as the one who drew his sword in the garden, I believe there is another tone mixed with Peter's denial. Beneath that first superficial layer of fear is a deeper emotion; Kierkegaard calls it the "sickness unto death." Despair. Consider once again the course of the evening. At first Peter is called on to play the servant, a role he seems perfectly willing to take on himself. But in the course of the meal, he finds his usual place beside Jesus now occupied by Judas. Again, these are small, speculative pieces, but they have a cumulative force. Next, when Jesus makes the absurd offer of washing his feet, Peter only says what the others should have said, "This is not appropriate!" He is only seeking to preserve his Master's dignity, and for this he receives a stern rebuke. Then, on the way to the garden, Jesus prophesies that Peter will deny him. You can begin to sense that his grip on the fragile and fragmented reality he had constructed around Jesus is beginning to slip.

In the garden he is invited, along with James and John, to keep watch with Jesus. All three of them fail in their vigil, but only Peter is rebuked. Finally, as the soldiers move to arrest Jesus, Peter alone responds with a full measure of courage. He draws the sword that Jesus had earlier told them to purchase, even at the cost of their coats.

If any action should have proven once and for all his fidelity to Jesus, it was this. Yet once again, Peter is rebuked. Finally he is left standing, holding his bloody sword, watching Jesus allow himself to be bound and led away. Once we have this course of events clearly in mind, we can hear the deeper tone in Peter's denials. "I do not know the man." After all, Peter's Messiah would have slaves washing his feet, not the other way around. His Messiah would command the legions of angels to destroy his enemies. His Messiah would have drawn his own sword as well. Peter understood a king who would take up arms to kill his enemies. Never in his wildest dreams could he imagine a king who would die to save his enemies. The despair that settles over his heart will be so complete that even when he sees the empty tomb and the grave clothes lying in their folds, Peter will walk away "wondering what had happened" (Luke 24:12). At that point, his despair would not allow him to trust Jesus' own word that he would rise on the third day.

So extreme will be the turnaround in his emotional life after seeing the risen Lord that he will throw himself into the lake and swim a hundred yards just to be close to him once again. But for now that is an eternity away.

One of the subtle indications that the Gospel of Mark came largely from the preaching of Peter is that, most often, when he is portrayed it is in humility or downright humiliation. Peter will not allow Mark to hide the failure of his denials, but there is still an incredible omission in Mark's version of the story as well as all the other Gospels except Luke. Upon Peter's third denial, only Luke tells us that Jesus turned and looked at Simon across the courtyard. As their eyes met, Peter remembered Jesus' prediction that he would deny him. It was, I believe, this look that broke Peter's heart.

The Gaze

Luke uses a specific word for Jesus' glance. It is, interestingly enough, the same word John used to describe the very first time Jesus looked at Peter. It is the Greek word *emblepō*. Jesus uses it when he tells the disciples to "consider" the lilies of the field. It means to see with your mind, to understand. It is sometimes translated "look straight at." But this fails to capture the force of this moment.

The understanding gaze of Jesus could not have been one of disdain or condemnation. That was not Jesus' way. After all, Jesus would be condemned for Peter. I believe the only look that could have broken Simon as it did was one of love and forgiveness. Which is just what we would expect from the Savior.

Upon first seeing him, Jesus knew all there was to know about Simon, the son of Jonah. He was able to give him in that first meeting (according to John's Gospel) his prophetic title, *Cephas*, the Rock. And just now, seeing Peter at his absolute worst, Jesus is willing to turn and go to the cross for Peter—and for you and me. After all, he sees us just the same way as he first did Peter. He gazes at us with that understanding stare and sees all our potential, all our frailties and faults. And yet he was willing, even while we were still sinners, to take up that cross for us. If, every time we read these passages about the failure and heartbreak of Peter, our hearts don't at the same time break a little more, we have failed to interact with the details of Scripture at the level of our imaginations.

That's one of the wonderful qualities about having our corporate identity in someone like Simon. He is us! Jesus could have chosen no one better. Even as he cried out when he began to sink into the sea, so now as he begins to sink into his own despair Peter goes out and weeps bitterly. He cries once more and will once more be rescued and forgiven by Jesus. Though we can know for certain that he was completely forgiven, one wonders if he ever completely forgave himself.

There is one more interesting omission. At the conclusion of his version of the story, John simply says the cock crowed. He omits the heartbreak of Peter. Since he alone was there to witness this total breaking of his companion, it is not hard to understand why he could not find the words to tell us about it.

CHAPTER TWELVE

". . . and Peter"

MARK 16:7

A significant fact about the resurrection of Jesus that, it seems to me, is seldom pointed out is simply this: no one, not a single one of his followers, expected him to rise from the dead! Mark tells us of the faithful women making their way to the tomb early in the morning, just after sunrise, with spices *to anoint a dead body.* Even when they see the stone rolled away, no one guesses that Jesus has risen. They assume that someone has taken the body. This must be figured into our equation if we are to understand everyone's emotional state that morning, especially Simon's.

The two Marys, along with Salome, wonder along the way who will move the stone for them. When they get to the tomb they discover they needn't have worried. Strong invisible hands have already rolled the heavy stone back. As they enter the tomb, expecting the worst, they encounter instead a young man dressed in white.

Before they have a chance to ask the obvious question, he says, "You are looking for Jesus of Nazareth, who was crucified. He has risen. He is not here." Then, almost as an afterthought, he says:

> But go, tell his disciples and Peter, "He is going ahead of you into Galilee. There you will see him, just as he told you." (Mark 16:7 NIV)

It is significant that only Mark records this detail. It was the first hint to Peter that everything had been made right. He was still included. He was forgiven. The One whom he had denied would not deny Simon Peter.

John tells us that Mary then ran to Peter and John to tell them the good news, the best of all news. Luke alone says that the women's words sounded like nonsense to the disciples but apparently not so nonsensical to Peter, who, Luke says, then ran to the tomb. In his Gospel, John lets us know that he also was a part of that early morning race. In fact, he, being younger, won!

When they arrive, John hesitates at the tomb door, like any good Jewish boy, not wanting to contract uncleanness. Peter, who, we will later see, was as scrupulously observant as any of the others, heedlessly enters the tomb. Then come the tantalizing details of the interior of the tomb that all the Gospel writers feel a need to record. The grave clothes were "lying in their folds" while the *sudorion,* or sweat cloth that covered Jesus' face, was folded up separately by itself. The tomb was empty. Surely Peter remembered Jesus' repeated words about rising again? Whatever the reason,

Luke then records one of the most staggering and yet telling details about Simon's state of mind. He says Peter "went away, wondering to himself what had happened" (24:12 NIV). John records that the sight was enough to convince him. "He [John] saw and believed" (20:8).

It was that same old lesson again. The one Jesus had first sought to teach Peter when he was caught in the storm. And then again when he walked on the water but sank. Jesus had made the point countless times. In one sense it might have been his most important lesson, apart from teaching them who he was. They had needed to hear it again and again, even as we require hearing it over and over. The lesson: the call of Jesus is for Peter to look beyond what might seem to be the reality of the situation to a new dimension of faith.

There was, after all, only one real possibility—the body had been stolen by any one of a number of men who wanted to thwart Jesus' mission. What Peter had smelled drifting from the tomb of Lazarus was reality. The gravity that pulled him back down toward the bottom of the lake was reality. And the empty tomb could speak only one reality to them that morning. But there is a mustard seed of faith in Simon's heart, and so the fact that he was "wondering to himself what had happened" should encourage us. At least he was wondering!

In as little as a few hours Peter will have presented before him the embodiment of this new reality. In resurrected flesh and bone and blood Jesus will stand before them all. He will encourage them to touch him and understand the warm reality of his resurrection. He will even eat a piece of fish for them, almost like a parlor trick, to show them that this—that he—is real. And because he is alive and real, everything he has promised them can be seen now to be true.

The Unrecorded Appearance

There is one more glaring omission that needs to be pointed out. If it should appear anywhere, it should be in Mark's Gospel. But it is nowhere to be seen there. Neither is it in Matthew or John. There is only the faintest hint of it in Luke. What I'm referring to is the first resurrection appearance to any of the disciples. And it was, of course, to Peter. It must have occurred sometime after Peter's "wondering" episode outside the tomb. Luke mentions it after the Emmaus Road appearance.

When the two men who have been speaking to Jesus on the road burst in on the disciples they blurt out, "It is true! The Lord has risen and has appeared to Simon" (Luke 24:34 NIV).

If this were the only mention we had of this mysterious appearance, we might be forced to try to make it fit the existing scheme of the postresurrection appearances in the Gospels. But Paul, a later friend and companion of Peter, mentions it as well. In 1 Corinthians he writes:

> He was buried, and he was raised from the dead on the
> third day, as the Scriptures said. He was seen by Peter
> and then by the twelve apostles. (1 Corinthians 15:4-5)

Where is the account of the content of this meeting? Why did Peter not give it to Mark? If John was nearby when it occurred, why did he not mention it? There seems to be no trace of it in Peter's letters either. The silence of the omission is deafening.

It is impossible to know the content of that first meeting. We can only guess. Peter never refers to his failure in denying Jesus again. (More than once Paul will make reference to his pre-Christian failures.) One wonders if together the two of them dealt with the denials so thoroughly that they never needed to be mentioned. I wonder too if perhaps Jesus himself might have commanded Peter not to mention it again, as he had told them before not to mention certain healings and revelations about who he was. Or could Jesus have appeared to Peter when he did because Peter was moving in the direction of Judas? Did Jesus save him again? We will never know.

Without a doubt, something deeply heart wrenching and emotional must have taken place between the two of them that everyone chose not to record. We can safely speculate that they somehow "dealt with" Peter's failure during that time together. It would have been aching in the forefront of Peter's heart. Perhaps he fell once more at Jesus' feet and confessed that he was not the man to lead the disciples.

Whatever the content of their meeting, we never again hear a word of Peter's denials. And when he next sees Jesus, he will be so unhindered in his emotions that he will throw himself into the lake and swim a hundred yards to shore just to be by his side. That was the act of a joyfully forgiven man. If Jesus had not been raised, Peter would have never known such forgiveness. And neither would, neither could, we.

CHAPTER THIRTEEN

A Farewell on the Seashore

JOHN 21:1-23

How many times had he walked back into their lives after a hopeless night of fishing? And now, this one last time, he appeared again. Their nets were once again empty, as empty as their hearts and souls. It was almost as if their last three years together had never really happened. Had they? Here they were, back where they started on the calm morning lake with empty nets after working all night. What was it he had said? Fishers of *men*?

Jesus appeared to Peter again where it all began three years earlier, on the shore of the lake. Peter, who was to fish for men, was fishing, unsuccessfully, once more for fish. It was almost as if nothing had happened. But all at once there he stood, not in glory with the legions of angels he said he commanded but by a waning fire he himself had built with those ruined hands. (They never got used to the sight of them.)

The fire, like their hopes, was about to go out. This was his third appearance to them. It was not the last.

Later Jesus appeared again to the disciples beside the Sea of Galilee. This is how it happened.

Several of the disciples were there—Simon Peter, Thomas (nicknamed the Twin), Nathanael from Cana in Galilee, the sons of Zebedee, and two other disciples.

Simon Peter said, "I'm going fishing."

"We'll come, too," they all said. So they went out in the boat, but they caught nothing all night.

At dawn the disciples saw Jesus standing on the beach, but they couldn't see who he was.

He called out, "Friends, have you caught any fish?"

"No," they replied.

Then he said, "Throw out your net on the right-hand side of the boat, and you'll get plenty of fish!" So they did, and they couldn't draw in the net because there were so many fish in it.

Then the disciple whom Jesus loved said to Peter, "It is the Lord!" When Simon Peter heard that it was the Lord, he put on his tunic (for he had stripped for work), jumped into the water, and swam ashore. The others stayed with the boat and pulled the loaded net to the shore, for they were only out about three hundred feet. When they got there, they saw that a charcoal fire was burning and fish were frying over it, and there was bread.

"Bring some of the fish you've just caught," Jesus said. So Simon Peter went aboard and dragged the net to the shore. There were 153 large fish, and yet the net hadn't torn.

"Now come and have some breakfast!" Jesus said. And no one dared ask him if he really was the Lord because they were sure of it. Then Jesus served them the bread and the fish. This was the third time Jesus had appeared to his disciples since he had been raised from the dead.

After breakfast Jesus said to Simon Peter, "Simon son of John, do you love me more than these?"

"Yes, Lord," Peter replied, "you know I love you."

"Then feed my lambs," Jesus told him.

Jesus repeated the question: "Simon son of John, do you love me?"

"Yes, Lord," Peter said, "you know I love you."

"Then take care of my sheep," Jesus said.

Once more he asked him, "Simon son of John, do you love me?"

Peter was grieved that Jesus asked the question a third time. He said, "Lord, you know everything. You know I love you." (John 21:2-17)

John, who loves to make significant omissions and substitutions to the story of Jesus, does it here one last time. Luke told us about the first miraculous catch of fish. John tells us about the last. The Gospels all record Peter's denials. Only John, Peter's gentle and loving friend since his childhood, records the threefold restoration of Peter. It is one of John's most kindly substitutions.

As usual, everyone has followed Peter's lead. "I'm going fishing," he says. And a number of them follow.

What else did they have to do while they awaited Jesus' promise about the coming Holy Spirit? After all, he had been coming and going from their lives for a score of days. Evaporating through locked doors, miraculously appearing with the equivalent of a simple "Hi" on his lips. And yet, though they "knew" it was Jesus, at the same time they didn't ever fully know. Mary thought he was the gardener. His familiar voice made her certain it was Jesus. The disciples on the road to Emmaus didn't recognize him either, even though they talked with him for hours about the promises in the Old Testament. Their eyes weren't opened till he broke the bread, and then he vanished once more. It was never his face he pointed to when he wanted them to recognize him. It was always his wounds. "Look, it's me," he would say with a sigh and a tired smile whenever he pointed to them.

This morning he shouts—perhaps mischievously?—to them, "Don't you even have a bite to eat?" (Expecting the answer "No.") "Throw your nets to starboard," he calls out.

"Why not," they mutter to themselves as they oblige the stranger.

And then it happens . . . again. Suddenly the boat lists hard to starboard and the ropes creak. Peter almost loses his footing. John bends over the side, both hands tight on the nets. Looking not at Jesus but at the fish-filled nets, he gasps, out of breath, "It's the Lord!" (If it weren't for the first miraculous catch he never would have recognized Jesus at the second.)

John's short gasping phrase is all Peter needed to hear. We do not hear Peter calling out, boldly asking if he might walk on the water. He gets to Jesus the best and fastest way he can. He throws his fisherman's coat on and dives into the chilly water. Does he wonder if he might walk again across the water? Is that why he jumps in with all his clothes on? Apparently John doesn't think we need to know. What is certain is that there was not a molecule of reluctance in Simon's heart. He *had* to get to Jesus. What's a hundred-yard swim in the cold morning water if it means being beside *him?*

Peter sprints from the water's edge, splashing everything, including Jesus, like some sort of retriever. He stands a few feet in front of him, bent at the waist, hands on his knees, terribly out of breath. He hesitates for two seconds and then enfolds Jesus in his cold, soaking embrace. There are tears in both their eyes. If it had been a hundred miles instead of a hundred yards, Peter would have still gladly crossed them for this moment. You see, every time Jesus appeared, Peter feared it might be for the last time.

By now the others have made it to the shore, towing the tremendous catch. Only now does Peter notice the smell of the bread and fish already cooking on the coals.

A few weeks earlier he might have protested, "Lord, you shouldn't have done this," but now he knows better. Jesus smiles at the others and invites them to bring along some of the fish they have caught. Peter turns and performs the herculean task of dragging the net to shore, all by himself!

They stand before Jesus in a loose semicircle, a strange expression on all their faces except Peter's. John tells us they're wondering to themselves, *Is it really him?* No, they knew it was Jesus. But was that after all really his face? No one dared ask (21:13).

The Final Meal

The meal was uncharacteristically quiet. There was little of the usual laughter, and certainly no one argued this time about who was the greatest. That had been settled. The greatest, they now understood, had just prepared their breakfast like a common servant though he was the risen Lord of Glory. The lesson was not wasted on Peter especially. He, quite uncharacteristically, seems to have had nothing to say.

When they were finished Jesus looked as if he had something important to say. He always became quiet and looked down for a few moments just before he would begin to teach them. Peter was just getting dry by this time. The fish and bread, along with no sleep that night, were just catching up with him when the sound of his name startled him.

"Simon, son of John," Jesus said, "Do you truly love me more than these?"

Peter had not said a word. He had only been sleepily looking around at the different faces in the firelight. Only the jolt of Jesus' question made him realize that inwardly he was indeed, once again, comparing himself to the others and affirming secretly inside that he loved Jesus the most. Had anyone else dived in and swum to him?

"Yes, Lord, you know that I love you," Peter responded without looking up. Jesus had used the word *agapaō* when he asked about Peter's love. Peter responded with another Greek word for love, *phileō*. Too much has been made of the differing words. John uses the different words in order to capture the varying tone of their exchange. Almost certainly they did not speak Greek anyway. Peter's word was also used by John in recording Jesus' statement of the Father's love for him (5:20), so how could that be categorically seen as inferior to *agapaō*?

The first call to become fishers of men had come there beside the sea. Now comes the call to be a shepherd. "Then feed my lambs," Jesus says, looking up into Peter's tired face. Peter might secretly think his love for Jesus is superior to all others. Perhaps it even was. But love is seen only in obedience. Even as Jesus has just fed them fish and bread, as indeed he has been feeding them for three years, so now Peter is to take the lead in feeding the lambs. And what is he supposed to feed them? Why Jesus, of course.

A second time Jesus asks. Peter is slightly pricked by the second question. "You know that I love you," he responds. If by now he knows anything about Jesus, Simon knows he can see inside a person's heart to its very core.

"Take care of my sheep," Jesus responds. Sheep, like people need to be both fed and tended. That is the complete role of the shepherd. That will be the complete responsibility of Peter and all the apostles. "Shepherd" will became a major category for Peter in his letters (1 Peter 2:25; 5:2, 4). After all, that is what the word "pastor" means.

John does not tell us how much time went by before Jesus asked the third and final question. Sometimes I imagine it was several minutes, enough for Peter to have forgotten the flow of the conversation. However long it was, when the final question came, Peter understood that Jesus was making a point. Three times the question had come. Three times Peter had denied him.

Jesus is not only the perfect Savior; he is also the perfect Friend. And here he demonstrates perfectly what friendship entails. He has commanded them to forgive; now he will perfectly demonstrate it. His painful questions are meant to restore Peter to his proper place. Painful as the questions are, they are an expression of Jesus' creative forgiveness. Jesus' questions open a wound in Peter's soul, a wound that can be tended to and healed only by being reopened.

The forgiveness Jesus has commanded them to offer has been offered to them, and it empowers Peter. Now he understands that his position of leadership is founded not on his strength but on his brokenness. Jesus had said of the woman, "I tell you, her sins—and they are many—have been forgiven, so she has shown me much love. But a person who is forgiven little shows only little love" (Luke 7:47). If that was still true, then Peter's love must be the greatest because he has been forgiven of the greatest sin. Even in this Peter ranks first among the disciples. Once it is firmly established in his heart, he will be fit to lead them.

"You know everything, Lord; you know that I love you," a broken Simon says to the One whom he knows sees every hidden corner of his heart. Notice that Peter's position of leadership is based not on faith but on love. His faith has failed him more times than either of them can count, but his love has been constant, powerful, even if occasionally misguided.

It all took place beside a coal fire. The last time Peter had stood beside such a fire it was in despair and denial. Now it is a new world. And yet we can't help thinking that the smell of the coals in his nose was powerful reminder of what had happened only a few days ago. Forgiveness, restoration and the new privilege of a new call.

> Jesus said, "Then feed my sheep. The truth is, when you were young, you were able to do as you liked and go wherever you wanted to. But when you are old, you will stretch out your hands, and others will direct you and

take you where you don't want to go." Jesus said this to let him know what kind of death he would die to glorify God. Then Jesus told him, "Follow me." (John 21:17-19)

Jesus' command is clear. There is no longer any misunderstanding on Simon's part. The remainder of his life will be spent living out Jesus' words. He will become the primary shepherd of the little, frightened flock of believers. He will care for them, risking his life to fend off the wolves. And he will feed them on Jesus' word.

Sandwiched between the final calls "Feed my sheep" and "Follow me," Jesus gives to Peter what all of us want and do not want at the same time: a prophecy of his own death. Jesus knows that in time Peter will need the kind of confidence that only this sort of word can give. His death, when it finally comes, will have been foreseen by Jesus decades earlier. Jesus does not only know that Peter will die, he knows how.

The key phrase of Jesus' prophecy is "stretch out your hands." In those words Peter would have heard without a doubt a reference to crucifixion. Epictetus wrote, "Stretch yourselves out like men who have been crucified" (*Disc* 3.26.22). Seneca spoke of "others stretching out their arms on a cross beam" (*Consol ad Marciam* 20:3) The two terms most often used to refer to crucifixion were "to be lifted up" and "to be stretched out." Peter would be crucified like Jesus, only when the time came, having had all these years to think about it, he would beg to be "stretched out" upside down. He did not feel worthy to die like Jesus.

They had first met beside this very same sea, on this same shore. At first Jesus had to show Simon that the lake he thought was empty was indeed full of fish. Now he has done it once again. Now a new kind of fisherman is left standing there—beside not a lake of fish but a vast sea of souls. He will fish for men and women. He will tend and feed the flock of Jesus. He can accomplish all this now because, in his brokenness, he knows the certainty both of his love for Jesus and—more importantly—of Jesus' love for him. He is armed with the painful knowing of his own end. He is ready.

Part Two

THE BRIDGE

CHAPTER FOURTEEN

The Passionate Preacher

ACTS 1—15

As I attempt to write this section, I am in Budapest at a missionary conference sponsored by the Moody Bible Institute. God's timing never ceases to amaze me. At precisely the time when I need a fresh understanding of what it means to be called as a missionary, he places me in the midst of eight hundred missionaries from all over Europe! If I am to come to understand the later ministry of Peter, it will not be from a book, it will be here in the midst of these remarkable brothers and sisters.

As I listen to the struggles of different missionaries on the field, I am reminded in each instance how Peter's experience was so much the same. One brother shared the story of his wife being killed while seeking only to love Arab women for the gospel's sake. I realize as I listen to his tears that Peter lost loved ones as well as he sought to follow Jesus. If one record can be trusted, he witnessed the death of his wife as well.

Someone else told of the heartbreak of leaving home again and again. As best I understand it, this was Peter's experience too. At least during Jesus' life and ministry, he maintained his house in Capernaum. The Twelve came back again and again only to leave once more, though after Jesus' death, as the scope of his ministry became vastly broader, he may have pulled up roots altogether. The details of this we cannot know for certain.

Another sister spoke of the danger of arrest she faced simply for telling others about Jesus. I remembered as I listened to her that Peter found himself in prison for Jesus at least three times. The rejection by family and religious leaders, the danger of persecution and death—these Peter and the disciples had faced when Jesus was present with them. Now, as they passed from the world of having Jesus, the perfect leader, in their midst, to being led by numerous decidedly imperfect leaders, they were no doubt comforted by the truth that they could not suffer any pain that Jesus had not already experienced.

It required someone special to bridge that divide. Peter was that bridge. And, paradoxically, he was also the first to cross over into this new situation of Jesus' physical absence and spiritual presence.

Peter in Acts

George Eliot once said, "It is never too late to be what you might have become." This is precisely the process we see at work in the life of Simon Peter in the second volume of Luke's two-part work, Luke-Acts. Simon, by grace, grows into the Rock Jesus prophesied he would become.

Though the name Simon occasionally reappears (Acts 10:5, 32;

15:14 NIV), he now takes on his title as a proper name. Henceforth he will be called simply Peter. He provides a living link to Jesus of Nazareth for the early church.

In the first twelve chapters of Acts, once again Peter is clearly the star and the leader of the church, the first preacher, the first apologist and the first healer.

- We see him presiding over the appointment of Matthias (chap. 1).

- He explains to the crowd the mystery of the Pentecost event and gives the first sermon (chap. 2).

- He performs the first healing in like manner to Jesus (chap. 3).

- When Peter and John are seized, Peter alone explains their actions. John is completely silent (chap. 4).

- It is Peter who handles the tragic case of Ananias and his wife.

- Though Luke tells us "the apostles healed many," it is Peter's shadow the crowd desires to have fall on them (chap. 5).

- When Peter and John are confronted by Simon the sorcerer, only Peter speaks and rebukes him (chap. 8).

- Peter heals Tabitha and Aeneas (chap. 9).

- It is Peter who first reaches out to the Gentiles (chap. 10).

- When he is criticized for "breaking the rules," he articulates for the first time this new dimension into which God is taking the church. (chap. 11).

- And finally, in chapter 12, Herod arrests Peter, after having killed James. An angel rescues Peter and he—we are simply told—"left for another place."

Though he will reappear briefly one final time at the

Jerusalem council in chapter 15, chapter 12 effectively marks his exit as character and prime focus of the narrative. Our task of looking at this phase of his ministry will be manifestly easier now, since we will have only Luke's record in Acts to examine.

Interrupted Sermons

It has been my experience that some of the best sermons are the interrupted ones. My close friend and pastor Denny Denson was in the middle of a sermon one Sunday morning when he saw a young man he had been witnessing to for months on the street slip into the back of the church. He was a victim of crack cocaine and had more than once tried to get off the drug, promising to some-day attend our church. Needless to say, when Denny saw him walk in that morning he was hopeful and excited that he had come.

After a few minutes the young man got up and walked back outside. Denny understood at once what he needed to do. He stopped in the middle of his sermon and asked the congregation to go to prayer. With that he followed the man outside and caught up with him a block down from the church. After perhaps fifteen minutes the two of them came back inside with good news. The young man had finally accepted Jesus as his Lord and Savior. The remainder of the service was spent in worship. He never finished the sermon!

We hear Simon Peter preach a total of four sermons in the book of Acts. (His first address to the believers in regards to the replacement of Judas in 1:15-25 is more a matter of church order than a formal sermon.) The first two sermons are complete (2:14-40; 3:12-26). The second two are both interrupted, one by the angry, frustrated elders (4:8-12, resumed in 5:29-32), and the final one by the Holy Spirit (10:34-43). Fragmented though they might be, we will see that the two interrupted sermons were both used by God to further his purposes. What a lesson for us today who are so committed to completing our schedules and finishing our outlines!

When Peter remembered the first time he ever heard Jesus preach in the synagogue just down the street from his home in Capernaum, the emotion he recalled was "amazement" (Mark 1:27). The people were amazed by the authority and freshness of Jesus' preaching. He did not teach like the rabbis, whose erudition was demonstrated by the list of rabbinic sayings they could quote on any of an impressive number of subjects. No, Jesus simply spoke the truth. If he quoted anyone it was God himself.

When the authorities would later hear the formally uneducated Peter and his companions preach and recall the passion and authority they had heard only once before from the Nazarene, the authorities would remember that these men had "been with Jesus" (Acts 4:13). But right now Jesus had been gone barely seven weeks, and it was Peter's turn to speak the words of God and do his work.

Peter's sermons follow a loose four-part pattern. This structure seems to me more the result of the order of his thinking about the message of Jesus and less a matter of slavishly sticking to a formal pattern that he had committed to memory. The structure is as follows. First, there would be the announcement that the days of fulfillment of God's purpose had arrived (Acts 2:14-21; 3:11; 4:8-11; 10:34-36). Second, he would give a brief overview of the life, death and resurrection of Jesus (2:22-24; 3:13-21; 4:10-12; 10:37-42). Third would be the confirmation of the Old Testament witnesses (2:25-35; 3:22-25, interrupted; 10:43) Fourth and finally would come the call to repent of their personal complicity in the death of Jesus (2:36-40; 3:26; 4:29-32, interrupted).

Pentecost Apologia

Peter's first sermon (Acts 2:14-40), and by far his longest, comes as an apologia or explanation of the miracle of Pentecost. The multilingual, multinational crowd has just heard in at least sixteen different languages (and probably more) what they can only describe as the "wonders of God." The specific content of what they heard "in their own languages" from the lips of the Galilean disciples is not recorded in the text. In effect, the content of the sermon the Holy Spirit was preaching through the disciples was not so much the point. The point was that God had now chosen to literally dwell in his people. To Luke the wonder or miracle was not so much what their ecstatic utterances said; it was the clear reversal of the Old Testament curse of Babel (Genesis 11:1-9).

The New Age that Peter would proclaim at the opening of his sermons had clearly come. The Spirit had returned in power, like a violent wind. The presence of the Lord that had departed in the time of Ezekiel had at last returned (Ezekiel 10:18). It had not returned to fill a temple, however; the tongues of fire above each of the disciples' heads signified that they had all become living tabernacles. Moses' prayer in Numbers 11:29 was coming true. God was pouring his Spirit on all his people.

Earlier, when God had spoken to encourage his Son, some of

the people who heard the voice had mistaken it for thunder (John 12:29). Again here, the people are unable to grasp what the Lord is saying through this mysterious outpouring. Some of them try to write it off as just so many drunkards under the influence. In response to the confusion, Peter stands up and preaches his first sermon in Acts. He begins, as he will begin all his sermons in Acts, by announcing that the days of the fulfillment of God's purpose have arrived. He quotes an extensive passage from the prophet Joel, presumably from memory! In his preaching as well as his two letters, Peter will evidence an impressive grasp of the Old Testament.

Next he moves on to the second part of his sermon, a brief account of the ministry of Jesus of Nazareth. He will almost always tell the story in such a way as to remind his listeners that they were accomplices in the nailing of Jesus to the cross. He was "handed over to you," Peter reminds them, who, "with the help of wicked men," crucified him.

Then follows a series of Old Testament quotes centering on David as a source. He had foreseen the resurrection, that Jesus would not be "abandoned to the grave," nor would he "undergo decay." Peter remembered a psalm he had once heard Jesus quote to confuse the Pharisees (Luke 20:42-44). Now seemed a good moment to bring it forth again. The resurrected one was the very same person David had called Lord in Psalm 110:1. Peter brings this penultimate part of his sermon to a close with a powerful charge, "God has made this Jesus whom you crucified both Lord and Christ!" Peter must have summoned all the passion he could muster in the tone of this final statement. Its impact on the crowd makes it clear. Luke tells us they were pierced (or stung) to the heart and cried out, "What shall we do?"

Their desperate response leads to the final section of Peter's first sermon. They must repent—turn completely around—and be baptized in the name of the very person they had a hand in nailing to the cross. Then, Peter tells them, they will receive the gift of the Holy Spirit, the very gift that has caused the entire ruckus in the first place.

This amazing promise is for them, for their children and for all who are far off, whom the Lord will call. At this early point in the ministry, there was no way Peter could see that the promise would spread as far as it eventually would—that he would be called on to extend it even across the vast distance of race to the Gentiles. The promise Jesus had spoken just before he had been taken up into heaven, that they would receive power and that they would become witnesses in Jerusalem, in all Judea and Samaria even to the ends of the earth, had begun to come literally true. The ever widening rings of the Spirit's influence, moving out, convicting, filling, saving, had now begun. The hundred and twenty who had huddled around Peter and the Eleven instantly became three thousand that morning in Jerusalem.

"Unpacking" a Miracle

Peter's second sermon occurred some time later (some commentaries say a few days; at least one says it might have been two years), also in response to a miracle. Peter and John were still observing the three o'clock time of prayer at the temple. (We will see in 10:3 that Cornelius, as a "God-fearer," also observed this time of prayer.) It is important to note that they were going to the temple to pray and not to make sacrifices. For them the Sacrifice had finally and forever been offered!

As Luke describes the event, they are passing through the gate that is called "Beautiful," the largest and main gate to the temple area, richly fashioned out of Corinthian bronze. Since this was the main thoroughfare to the temple, beggars would congregate there en masse. Giving money to the poor was an intricate part of temple worship. Sadly, this cannot be said of the church today, when we so narrowly define worship. Though Peter and John were following the rest of the crowd into the temple, they were in the footsteps of Jesus!

When the lame man notices the two disciples, he calls out to them his well-rehearsed phrase. They turn and compassionately confront him. "Look at us!" Peter says. "Give us your attention. Do not regard us as simply sources of charity. We have infinitely more to give."

Standing beneath the extravagantly bronzed gate, Peter confesses he has no money, no silver or gold to give the poor man. He and John are likewise penniless beggars, like the crippled man, only they know Someone—and he is the wealth they have to give. "In the name of Jesus of Nazareth, walk!" Peter says. Like Jesus, when Peter exercises the healing authority he has been given he does not call attention to himself. There is no waving of arms in the air, no magical incantations, only the pronouncement of a loving and authoritative word. Instantly the man's feet and ankles regain their strength and he leaps to his feet, jumping and praising God. It's the scene from Mark 2 all over again, only this time

Jesus is not physically present to heal the lame. He is present in Peter and John, his obedient apostles. Isaiah's prophecy has come alive once more: the lame are leaping like deer (Isaiah 35:6). Whenever Jesus healed the sick, remarkably, the people always responded not by praising him but by giving praise to God. The humble, selfless way Jesus worked his miracles won praise not for himself but for his Father. The same goes for Peter.

We are told the man praises not Peter and John but God. He recognizes that the power that has healed his lame ankles is not the possession of the simple man who has spoken Jesus' name; the power is in the name itself!

As at Pentecost, the miracle causes a commotion that needs to be explained. And Peter's second sermon provides that *apologia*. The pattern we saw in his first sermon is repeated, but the content is fresh and completely different.

The miracle itself was an announcement that the time had come, and so it helps to fulfill the function of the first section of Peter's sermon. As the people run toward Peter and John, Peter immediately directs the attention away from themselves and toward the one whose power actually healed the man, Jesus. It was not their own power or godliness that made the healing happen, he says.

As he moves into the second section of his sermon, Peter begins his account of the ministry of Jesus, focusing particularly on his trial, conviction and death. He reaffirms what the Gospels make clear, namely, that Pilate was determined to let Jesus go. He tried to appease the crowd by flogging Jesus (even though he was innocent). He offered them a choice between Jesus and Barabbas. Pilate more than once said that they should take Jesus and judge him according to their own law. But that was not a sufficient answer for the priests because they could not execute Jesus; only the Romans possessed that authority. Pilate also tried to pass Jesus off to Herod, who was pleased to see him and have a magic trick or two performed for him. Pilate longed to listen to the troubling dreams his wife had been suffering concerning Jesus, but a voice from the crowd had threatened recriminations, and Pilate had relented. His own governorship was resting on a slippery slope since his patron, Sejanus, had lost his authority and his head.

But Peter's point still stands: the Roman governor had wanted to release Jesus, but the people had insisted not. Peter's point is that now they must face their own guilt in the matter (even as each of us must eventually face our own).

Peter's gift for words is displayed in the poetic tension of his presentation of Jesus' innocence in contrast to their guilt. Jesus, he says, was the Just One, but they had screamed out for the murderer Barabbas instead. Though he was the Prince of Life, they had killed him. But God had raised him from the dead! In anticipation of the fourth and final point of his sermon he urges them to "repent and be converted."

The third portion of Peter's sermons always provided an Old Testament confirmation of the reality of Jesus' life and ministry. Starting with verse 22, Peter appeals to Moses and one of the defining images of Jesus in the Pentateuch, "the Prophet like Moses." The people had occasionally wondered out loud if Jesus was this person (John 6:14; 7:40). The qualifying characteristic of the prophet was that he, like Moses, would speak only what God had told him to say. Jesus, again and again, especially in the Gospel of John, makes this exact statement about himself (John 8:14; 12:49; 14:10, 24).

Peter closes his Old Testament section with an appeal to all the prophets from Samuel on. He reminds his hearers that they are the sons both of the prophets and of the covenant that God made with the forefathers. God promised Abraham that through his seed all the nations of the world would be blessed. That promise of blessing has been fulfilled in every minute detail in the life and death of Jesus of Nazareth.

All that is left is the challenge to repent. This Peter represents as the very act of God himself, who "raised up his servant, [and] sent him . . . to bless you by turning each of you back from your sinful ways" (Acts 3:26). In other words, what each one of his hearers was sensing in his or her own heart was in fact the activity of the God who raised Jesus from the dead.

Luke gives us no word on the response of the crowd to Peter's second sermon. Perhaps he assumes that, like the first sermon, the response was a guaranteed success. The people would once more be cut to the heart and repent, believing in Jesus. Perhaps, for literary or dramatic effect, he leaves their response silent to allow for the abrupt interruption of the temple officials who break in on the scene. A few verses later he will finally inform us that the response to this sermon caused the numbers of the disciples of Jesus to swell from three to five thousand! Josephus tells us that at this time there were only six thousand Pharisees living in Jerusalem. It is not difficult to imagine the pressure that the young and growing church was beginning to feel.

More Interrupted Sermons

Peter and John are seized by a three-part group: the priests, the captain of the temple guard (a Levite who was next in authority to the high priest himself) and the Sadducees. We are told that because it was evening they were placed in jail until the morning.

The next morning an amazing assembly of the most powerful men in the country comes together to hear what Peter and John have to say for themselves. Luke is careful to present the impressive roster. Annas is there, the high priest emeritus and father-in-law to Caiaphas, who was appointed in A.D. 18. John, or Jonathan, was present, the man who would succeed Caiaphas as high priest. We are told that Alexander was also there. His importance has been lost to history, except that he too was a part of the family of the high priest.

The court cannot condemn Peter and John for what they did. There was certainly no law against healing someone. So they take the direction of asking "by what authority or name" the disciples had done what they had done. Their hope is no doubt that the disciples will simply answer "Jesus of Nazareth" (which they eventually will). But Peter, filled with the Holy Spirit, does not provide a quick answer. He begins to preach to them. Jesus had promised that they would be given the words to speak when they were hauled in front of officials (Luke 21:13-15). This is the first example of that promise coming true.

Peter begins, as he always does, with the announcement that a new time is breaking in on them all. The one they crucified, whom God raised from the dead, is alive and still at work through his disciples. The act of kindness and healing of the cripple was actually the work not of Peter and John but of Jesus of Nazareth!

Certainly Peter understands that this is not a sympathetic audience. These, after all, are the very ones who condemned Jesus only a short time ago, in this very room! He knows that if he is to get his message out to them he must not mince words. And so Peter tries to move quickly on to the second section, the account of the ministry of Jesus. Once again there is a fresh presentation. He attempts to lay the scriptural groundwork for a presentation of Jesus as the Scandalon, the stumbling stone, whom they had only recently rejected. Peter quotes a passage he remembers Jesus using (Mark 12:10-11), a passage he will use again in his first letter (1 Peter 2:4-10). Simon, the one Jesus called the Rock, clearly understands that Jesus too is a stone.

Perhaps because he senses the nervous impatience of his listeners, Peter makes what he thinks will be his last point before the elders. Jesus is the only source of healing (the same word is used for "salvation" and "healing"). There is no other name by which people can be either healed or saved. It is difficult to remember that Peter and John are on trial here. Peter's words are not in the least a defense of either one of them. Instead, they are clearly on the offensive. They are attacking with the Truth!

Luke makes clear that the result of Peter's fragmented sermon is astonishment in his august listeners. They are astonished that unschooled men can speak with such courage and passion. But then they make an important connection. They remember that these men have been with Jesus!

Peter's "defense" leaves them literally speechless. Besides, the man he healed only the day before is standing there with them.

What can they possibly say?

The disciples are ordered to withdraw while the council confers. "Everyone in Jerusalem knows they have done an outstanding miracle," they whisper to one another, "so we can't deny it!" Interestingly, they make a decision based on the confidence they have in their own authority. They will order these men not to speak in Jesus' name anymore. That will certainly stop the spread of this new teaching. Little do they understand what real authority is.

They drag Peter and John back before the council and command that they stop speaking Jesus' name. It is then that the simple fisherman, the "unschooled" Peter, responds by quoting Plato's *Apology 29 D* where Socrates says, "Judge for yourselves whether it is right in God's sight to obey you rather than God." We cannot know if Peter ever read Plato, but we can see that at this point he was definitely thinking like Plato!

It was such a short time ago that in Caiaphas's own courtyard Peter had denied knowing Jesus at all. Now, in the broadest daylight, he courageously confesses that he cannot help himself. He must speak about all the things he has heard and seen. He will not refrain from speaking Jesus' name. How could he? Only Luke told us about Jesus' prayer for Peter, that he would turn and   strengthen his brothers (22:31-32). Here Luke presents the wonderful answer to that prayer. The two disciples are threatened once more but finally released. Peter will have another chance, a few days later, to finish the sermon that has been so rudely interrupted.

The church was encouraged by the release and apparent vindication of the apostles. As their numbers grew, so did the depth of their generosity and love. Luke tells us that they met together in a corner of the temple complex known as Solomon's colonnade. Here they openly practiced the compassion of Jesus through healing everyone who was brought to them as well as casting out demons. It was here that the superstitious began to seek to merely have Peter's shadow pass over them. As happened during the ministry of Jesus, the people confused the gifts the disciples had to offer with the real substance of what they most wanted to give. They were not, after all, simply healers. They had come to give the people Jesus. Today the same phenomenon is evident in the large crowds who flock only to receive a gift but remain essentially uninterested in really coming to know Jesus.

Luke lets us know that the cumulative weight of all this attention caused the high priests and his associates to become jealous. Mark says it was basically this same jealously that caused them to crucify Jesus (Mark 15:10). This time it is not only Peter and John but all the apostles who are rounded up and put into the public jail. During the night, for the first but not the last time, an angel opens the doors of the prison and charges them to tell the "full message of the new life," lest persecution might tempt them to leave the more scandalous parts out.

Once more the most powerful leaders gather, along with the full assembly of the elders, and call to have the prisoners brought forth from the prison. But the jail is empty, though the doors are all locked and the unassuming guards are still at their posts.

"Look!" someone shouts. "They're in the temple courts teaching the people!" Just what they were commanded by the high priest's authority not to do.

The captain and his temple guard politely ask the disciples if they would be willing to come to the assembly. Though Peter and the others might have played to the sympathies of the crowd, instead they keep the peace and humbly comply.

Once again before the assembly, Peter (and the others) give the same reason they voiced in chapter 4: "We must obey God rather than men!"

What follows sounds so remarkably like Peter's preaching that we must assume that it is Peter speaking once again. (We even hear him use his characteristic term for the cross, "tree," which he also uses in his first letter [1 Peter 2:24 NIV].) This brief sermonic clip seems to be an introduction for his fourth section. In other words, Peter takes up where he left off. He doggedly means to present his final appeal to the Sanhedrin! But these words are more than they can bear. Luke reports that they were furious and wanted to execute them then and there. It is then that one of the most remarkable men in Judaism takes the stage.

His name is Gamaliel, grandson of Rabbi Hillel, the founder of one of the two major schools of the Pharisees (the school, incidentally, with which Jesus most often sided). He had been one of Paul's teachers as well (Acts 22:3). He stands up and, against all popular sentiment in the Sanhedrin, makes a powerfully persuasive argument for letting the disciples go, lest they all be found "fighting against God." He makes the remarkable suggestion that the followers of Jesus might in fact be right! Had anyone else but the revered Gamaliel spoken up for them at this time, it would have been over. There is little doubt that many of the disciples would have been executed. One wonders if perhaps even Paul himself may have been present. There is little doubt that if he was, he would have vehemently disagreed with his teacher.

Though none of them were murdered that morning, still their blood was spilled as the result of a cruel flogging. Undeterred, Luke says, they rejoiced and returned to their tasks of preaching and teaching with all the more passion. They continued to gather in the temple courts and what's more, started going door to door telling everyone "the good news that Jesus is the Christ." And all this from a fragmented, interrupted sermon.

The final sermon of Peter in Acts will also be interrupted before he can finish. At the opening of part three the Holy Spirit will move upon the hearts of Cornelius and his friends and family. Peter will report, "Just as I was starting to speak . . ." Before he could get his sermon out, the Holy Spirit showed up and stole the show! (The details of this final sermon we will examine when we come to the story of Cornelius.) Then Peter curiously quotes the words of the venerable Gamaliel, whom God has used to spare his life: "Who was I to think that I could oppose God!"

Indeed, who was he but a simple fisherman caught in the wondrous web of Jesus' will for his life. In his sermons, if we must call them that, we hear the unadorned passion of Simon's heart. There is not a drop of pretense or self-awareness. He is not trying to posture or impress or even ultimately "win" his audience. What we hear is the heartfelt desire of a man who wants to tell the truth, wants to tell us simply what he has heard and seen. When he goes about trying to communicate this wonderful message, he starts with the simplest truth about the good news: that it has come! He then simply tells us about Jesus, always appealing to the Scriptures that are as much life and breath to him as anything could be.

Finally, he will call out to his hearers and to us to turn around from the foolishness and sin we so recklessly follow to our destruction, to realize that as much as any of the three soldiers who stretched Jesus on the cross beam and hammered the spikes into his hands and feet, we are responsible for his hanging there.

CHAPTER FIFTEEN

The Compassionate Healer

ACTS 3:1-10; 9:32-42

Peter performs three healings in Acts that build on each other in dramatic intensity and detail. First, we see the healing of the nameless lame beggar (3:1-10). In 5:15 we read the statement of the crowd's desire to have Peter's shadow pass over them for healing, but no specific incidences of healing are reported, just the fact that everyone who came to Solomon's colonnade to be healed was healed.

The second and third instances occur back to back in Acts 9. The second healing has to do with a man named Aeneas. Luke, always a stickler for medical detail, tells us this man was paralyzed (vv. 32-35). The third and last account concerns a godly woman named Tabitha (*Dorcas* in Greek). She has died, and we are told that Peter comes to raise her from the dead (vv. 36-43).

In each instance it is important to see the striking parallels between the healings done by Peter and those done by Jesus in the Gospels. Some commentators try to discredit the accounts in Acts, saying they resemble too closely those in the Gospels to be authentic. Claims are made that the healings in Acts were simply made up and cast in the form of the Gospel miracles. Nothing could be further from the truth. When we understand that Acts is the story of the continuation of the ministry of Jesus *through* his disciples, particularly Peter and Paul, we see that they were only picking up where Jesus left off. Peter will make it abundantly clear that it is not his power or authority but Jesus' that heals in every instance.

We looked earlier at some of the details of the first account of the healing at the Beautiful gate. We saw that, like Jesus, Peter did not draw attention to himself but simply spoke Jesus' authoritative name and the lame man was healed. "In the name of Jesus of Nazareth, walk!" Like Jesus, Peter and the disciples were later inundated with people who were desirous only of healing.

Having already looked at the first account of the lame man at the Beautiful gate, let's focus on the two accounts in chapter 9. So much had happened since that first encounter with the beggar outside the temple. Peter had been imprisoned twice and miraculously released. He experienced flogging and went away from the ordeal rejoicing. He and John had made their first preaching tour of Samaria (8:25). Perhaps most significantly in the narrative of Acts, Saul appeared, trying to meet with the disciples, who were initially afraid of him before the intervention of Barnabas (9:26-27). Perhaps because Saul had finally come to faith, we are told that the church enjoyed a brief respite from persecution. Peter, it seems, took this opportunity to visit a few of the young churches.

"Tabitha, Get Up!"

In Acts 9:32 Luke tells us he came to Lydda, a city perhaps first visited by Philip (8:40). It was only eleven miles southeast of Joppa. The core membership of this young church was probably composed of Jewish believers who had fled the persecution in Jerusalem (8:1). This was a primarily Jewish settlement, although there seems to have been a small Gentile community as well. After the fall of Jerusalem, most of the prominent rabbis resettled in Lydda. Church tradition tells us that Paul's companion, the lawyer Zenas, became the first bishop of the church at Lydda.

When Peter arrived in the city, he discovered there a man named Aeneas who had been paralyzed for eight years. The paralyzed man was named after one of the heroes of Homer's *Iliad*. This is a strong indication that he was not a member of the Jewish community. It is not clear whether he was a part of the young church.

What is abundantly clear is Peter's unwavering attribution to Jesus of the healing power. "Jesus Christ heals you!" Peter says. His second statement is not so unambiguous. It lacks a clear subject in the Greek. Peter literally says "arrange" or "spread." The commentators are divided between "arranging" or "making up his bed," which would be roughly parallel to Jesus' command to pick up your bed, or spreading his table, which would be somewhat like Jesus' command to give someone who had been healed something to eat (Luke 8:55).

The impact of his healing was immediate and widespread. Everyone who lived in Lydda witnessed it, as well as those of the nearby village of Sharon. So clear had Peter been in his attribution of the miracle to Jesus that the townsfolk in both cities turned to the Lord. The account of this second healing by Peter is only three verses long and sparse in detail. But the third and final story is lengthy and filled with details:

> In Joppa there was a disciple named Tabitha (which in Greek is Dorcas). She was always doing kind things for others and helping the poor. About this time she became ill and died. Her friends prepared her for burial and laid her in an upstairs room. But they heard that Peter was nearby at Lydda, so they sent two men to beg him, "Please come as soon as possible!"
>
> So Peter returned with them; and as soon as he arrived, they took him to the upstairs room. The room was filled with widows who were weeping and showing him the coats and other garments Dorcas had made for them. But Peter asked them all to leave; then he knelt and prayed. Turning to the body, he said, "Get up, Tabitha." And she opened her eyes! When she saw Peter, she sat up! He gave her his hand and helped her up. Then he called in the widows and all the believers, and he showed them that she was alive.
>
> The news raced through the whole town, and many believed in the Lord. (Acts 9:36-42)

We discover that Peter made the short eleven-mile trip to Joppa (present-day Tel Aviv) at the request of some disciples there who had heard he was in nearby Lydda. They had just lost their sister in Christ, Tabitha, who was extremely dear to the community. We are told that she was always doing good and caring for the poor. When Peter arrives at the house, the weeping widows pitifully show him the clothing Tabitha had once made and presumably given to others who had none.

Peter, we are told, asks everyone to leave the room. He kneels in prayer for an undisclosed period of time. Afterward, he turns toward the "dead woman" and by name simply tells her to "get up." He calls everyone back into the room and presents her to them alive. Of the three healings in Acts that are comparable to those of Jesus in the Gospels, this is the most strikingly similar.

All three Synoptic writers tell the story of the raising of Jairus's daughter (Matthew 9:18-26; Mark 5:22-43; Luke 8:40-56). In each account Jesus is sent for, just as Peter was. In each account the room is cleared. In the Gospels the Three are asked to remain with the little girl's parents. In the story of Peter it seems he is completely alone with the corpse. The command of Jesus, "Little girl (*talitha*), get up," differs by only one letter from Peter's "Tabitha, get up." It is especially interesting to note that only in the Gospel of Mark, which reflects Peter's account of the story, is the word *talitha* used at all. Neither Matthew nor Luke use the term. Yes—if anyone would have been struck by the striking similarity of the events, it would have been Peter!

Peter's actions once more point to the fact that the raising of Tabitha was nothing more or less than a prayer Jesus chose to answer in the affirmative. In no way does Peter appropriate to himself any credit for the miracle. The result, once again, is seen in that many people all over Joppa put their faith in Jesus. Peter is not the focus of any adulation or attention.

As interestingly similar as the two events are, I find more interesting still what is different about them. In the story of Jairus's daughter, it is clear that Jesus is sent for while the girl is still alive. She dies while Jesus is making his way to her. One of the servants meets Jairus and Jesus on the way and makes a significant statement. After he has informed his master of the terrible news of the death of his daughter, he says, "Why bother the teacher any more." In other words, now that she is dead we might as well let Jesus go his way. There is nothing he or anyone could possibly do now. The same sentiment is seen in the story of Lazarus when both Martha and Mary accost Jesus with the words "*If only you had been here . . .*"

The implication is that now that death has come nothing can be done. No one expected that Jesus could raise the dead. Heal the sick, yes, but resurrection? Impossible!

Now look at the story in Acts. What is different about it? Clearly Tabitha is dead before Peter is sent for. Her body has been washed and prepared for burial. Nonetheless, Peter is sent for with a totally new expectation. Though there is no word of his having done this kind of miracle before, the Christians beside the sea in Joppa fully expect that he can do it precisely because *Jesus did it*.

Indeed, the New Age that Peter had been preaching about had come with an entirely new set of expectations. Already the truth of Jesus' life and resurrection had begun to take effect. Peter, who had stood by at the home of Jairus those many months ago, understood now and believed that because Jesus was alive and living in and through him in the person of the Holy Spirit, death had indeed lost its awful power. In Jesus it had become merely a sleep from which we will also someday awake when we hearing those same words, "Get up."

Awake, O sleeper, and arise from the dead, and Christ shall give you light. (Ephesians 5:14 RSV)

CHAPTER SIXTEEN

The Fearless Prisoner

ACTS 4:1-4; 5:18-20; 12:1-19

S omeone recently asked me to name my spiritual heroes. I mentioned Dietrich Bonhoeffer, Nicolae Moldoveanu, John Perkins and a man I met in China whom I only know as Brother John. When I looked at the list I realized that the only thing they all had in common was that each one had been in prison for his faith. A modern-day philosopher has said, "The only way to deal with an unfree world is to become so absolutely free that your very existence is an act of rebellion." In so fallen and "unfree" a world as we live in, is it any surprise that those who possess the glorious freedom of Christ so often end up in jail?

In Luke 22:33 Peter had protested to Jesus that he was willing to go to prison for him. At least three times he would have the opportunity to make good on that promise. In Acts we witness three increasingly severe and dangerous arrests and prison experiences in Peter's life. They will progress from simple detention for questioning to being held for execution. The first incident ended when the authorities released him. The last two imprisonments were miraculously brought to an end by an angel!

The first occasion, as we have already seen, was in connection with the first healing in Acts 3. Peter and John were held overnight by the captain of the temple guard. There was no formal charge. The purpose of their detention was so they could be questioned as to the details of their message concerning Jesus of Nazareth. They had been proclaiming the resurrection of Jesus from the dead. This first arrest became the setting for one of Peter's fragmented sermons before the council.

That he was preaching on the subject of Jesus was bad enough. The Nazarene had been convicted as a criminal, had died a humiliating death on the cross. Even during his lifetime a formal ban had been placed on Jesus (John 9:22). Anyone who associated with him would be cast out of the synagogue and out of Jewish life as well. To the Jewish mind, then as now, Jesus, a convicted criminal, was the last person who should be so revered and proclaimed.

Coupled with this was the added difficulty that they were also preaching resurrection. The Sadducees, who controlled the temple and the priesthood, having purchased the privilege from the Romans, did not believe in the resurrection. They were strict followers of the Torah and could find no reference to resurrection (or angels) in any of the books of Moses. It was certainly a coup when Jesus demonstrated to them from their own Torah that there was such a thing as life after death (Luke 20:27-40)!

This first experience of prison ended with a few threats and the command not to preach in Jesus' name any longer (Acts 4:18, 21). These threats were, of course, completely ignored by Peter and John. They were compelled by their passion for the good news of Jesus. Who could possibly be silent about such an awesome Lord?

Peter's next experience of prison came as a direct result of the jealousy the religious leaders felt toward him and the other disciples. The church numbered more than five thousand by this time. This means that they were coming close to outnumbering the Pharisees. In spite of the first warning they received, they continued meeting in the temple precincts and preaching the good news of Jesus in Solomon's colonnade. Several sick people were experiencing healing there as well. The detail that some were seeking simply to have Peter's shadow fall on them to be healed must have been particularly galling to the priests. In Judaism the passing over of the shadow could communicate uncleanness (if a leper was involved). In Jesus it had become the vehicle for communicating cleansing and healing! It is interesting that Peter remembered that it was this same sort of jealousy that led to the death of Jesus (Mark 15:10).

This time it is not only Peter and John who are arrested but all of the apostles. We are told they were placed in the public jail to be held overnight for a morning meeting before the Sanhedrin.

Sometime during the night a lone angel opens the gates of the prison and leads the Twelve outside. He gives them specific instruction to return to the temple courts and tell the people the "full message of this new life." Perhaps there was the chance that their persecution might tempt them to tell less than the full story, which of course would not be the true story at all. The next morning at daybreak they obey the angel—they take up their places in the temple courts and begin teaching anyone who will still risk listening to them.

Once the full council has convened, they send for the prisoners, only to hear back from the guards that the jail is empty, though the doors are all still securely locked! Luke whispers an ominous word from the guards when he tells us they wondered what would come of all this.

The disciples are finally located in the temple, where they continue to defy the order not to preach. The guards are sent to bring them before the council. This they do without force, which is understandable! Before the Sanhedrin, once more the disciples are confronted with their disobedience to a direct order from the high priest, the most powerful person in all Jerusalem. It would be tantamount to our disobeying a presidential order. In their charge to the disciples, the Jewish officials display a habit that will later become more firmly rooted in Judaism, namely the intentional avoidance of using the name of Jesus. Later in the Talmud he will be referred to as *peloni,* or "so-and-so."

"You are determined to make us guilty of this man's blood," they whine. Peter's habit of stressing their complicity in the death of Jesus in every one of his sermons is beginning to wear on their nerves or perhaps even their consciences.

Peter responds with the same idea he presented the last time they were detained (Acts 4:19). They are compelled to obey God rather than men. Peter's response to their question lights a fuse of anger that almost explodes in the disciples' faces. The council decides that they will deal with the Twelve precisely as they did with their master, Jesus. At this moment, as we saw earlier, Gamaliel stands up for the truth and incredibly defends the apostles before the Sanhedrin, saving their lives. This second imprisonment does not end simply with threats as the earlier one did. The disciples are ordered once more not to speak in Jesus' name—and to drive the message home, they are all flogged. Clearly the heat is being turned up.

The third and final imprisonment of Peter has a different character altogether. It is not the Sanhedrin who orders his arrest but Herod Agrippa, the grandson of Herod the Great. His hands were already bloodied by the death of James, the brother of John (Acts 12:2). He was the first of the apostles to die for Jesus' sake, having been told that someday he would indeed drink from the same cup as his Lord (Mark 10:39). Eusebius tells us that the soldier who executed him was so impressed by the way he died that he too became a believer and was executed.

The account is filled with eyewitness detail that could only have come from Peter himself.

> About that time King Herod Agrippa began to persecute some believers in the church. He had the apostle James (John's brother) killed with a sword. When Herod saw how much this pleased the Jewish leaders, he arrested Peter during the Passover celebration and imprisoned him, placing him under the guard of four squads of four soldiers each. Herod's intention was to bring Peter out for public trial after the Passover. But while Peter was in prison, the church prayed very earnestly for him.

The night before Peter was to be placed on trial, he was asleep, chained between two soldiers, with others standing guard at the prison gate. Suddenly, there was a bright light in the cell, and an angel of the Lord stood before Peter. The angel tapped him on the side to awaken him and said, "Quick! Get up!" And the chains fell off his wrists. Then the angel told him, "Get dressed and put on your sandals." And he did. "Now put on your coat and follow me," the angel ordered.

So Peter left the cell, following the angel. But all the time he thought it was a vision. He didn't realize it was really happening. They passed the first and second guard posts and came to the iron gate to the street, and this opened to them all by itself. So they passed through and started walking down the street, and then the angel suddenly left him.

Peter finally realized what had happened. "It's really true!" he said to himself. "The Lord has sent his angel and saved me from Herod and from what the Jews were hoping to do to me!"

After a little thought, he went to the home of Mary, the mother of John Mark, where many were gathered for prayer. He knocked at the door in the gate, and a servant girl named Rhoda came to open it. When she recognized Peter's voice, she was so overjoyed that, instead of opening the door, she ran back inside and told everyone, "Peter is standing at the door!"

"You're out of your mind," they said. When she insisted, they decided, "It must be his angel."

Meanwhile, Peter continued knocking. When they finally went out and opened the door, they were amazed. He motioned for them to quiet down and told them what had happened and how the Lord had led him out of jail. "Tell James and the other brothers what happened," he said. And then he went to another place.

At dawn, there was a great commotion among the soldiers about what had happened to Peter. Herod Agrippa ordered a thorough search for him. When he couldn't be found, Herod interrogated the guards and sentenced them to death.

Afterward Herod left Judea to stay in Caesarea for a while. (Acts 12:1-19)

It is a rich and very human story. Peter, being awakened by a whack on the side from the angel and then being led like a sleepy schoolboy to freedom, thinking all along that he is having a dream. Rhoda, the poor, confused servant, running off excitedly, leaving Peter dangerously exposed in the street. The Christians, who are praying so fervently for his release, not being willing to believe that their prayers have really been answered and Peter is outside the door.

But behind the charm of the account lies another layer of meaning—a deadly serious one. The innocent James has been murdered. It is a foretaste of things to come. Herod decides to take Peter simply to gain favor with the crowd. Kill Peter, kill Christianity. It was a simple, grim equation. That his death was certain is revealed in the consequence his escape has for the sixteen men responsible for guarding him. When Peter cannot be located, Herod orders that they be executed according to the Roman Code of Justinian, which dictated that if a prisoner escaped, the guard should receive the punishment his charge was to receive. This is reflected also in Acts 16:27, when Paul's jailer is about to fall on his own sword when he believes his prisoners have escaped after an earthquake.

Because of his miraculous release, Peter is given another thirty years to serve Jesus. He virtually disappears from the narrative at this point. He reappears briefly in chapter 15 at the Jerusalem Council. The added pressure of this final arrest and escape convinces him to leave Jerusalem, as so many other believers have already been forced to do, and become the missionary pastor he would be for the remainder of his life. Peter exits with the simple enigmatic phrase, "he left for another place."

Three experiences of prison. First threatened, then beaten and perhaps—like James—headed for death. In each instance Peter is unmindful of the danger to himself. The very fact that, on the night before what he knows will be his execution, he can sleep so soundly that it requires a sound angelic thump on the side to waken him, reveals the profound courage Jesus had instilled in his heart and mind. And when Peter is released that morning, some ten years after the liberation of Jesus from the tomb, he moves out from Jerusalem and never looks back. If the cold weight of the stone could not hold Jesus, then neither could the cruel iron bars of a prison cell. Peter experienced the freedom that all who have followed in his steps will testify to as well (1 Peter 2:16, 19-20). The call is to live as free men and women no matter the circumstances, no matter how "unfree" a world we find ourselves living in.

CHAPTER SEVENTEEN

The Reluctant Reconciler

ACTS 10:1-33

The first "black" church I attended was in Bowling Green, Kentucky. I was a student at Western Kentucky University, studying under Dr. William Lane. When I heard that he was preaching at a local church, I decided to check it out.

The first time I walked in the aged building and took a seat in the back, everything was unfamiliar to me. The songs were different than the ones I had known as a child. There were women deaconesses with white gloves taking up the offering. Though you might say that "in my flesh" I felt uncomfortable at first, still there was something in my spirit that resonated with the men and women whom I later considered some of my closest friends.

Twenty-five years later, where I live now in Franklin, Tennessee, I sensed the call to make the same sort of move, to cross the same line. Only this time there was not a white, Harvard-educated preacher in the pulpit. Neither were there other white people my same age. The church I felt called to, First Missionary Baptist, was all black. When I visited I was the only white person in the sanctuary. Though I had been meeting there for a year or more to pray with the men of the Empty Hands Fellowship (along with Dr. Lane), this was a different situation altogether.

As I walked in, an elderly woman came up to me and asked, "Why are you here?" It was not an angry question. She really wanted to know. And I could not give her a good answer. I could only stammer, "I'm a friend of Denny's."

I sat, once more in the back, in the only empty seat I could find. I was nervous. Several people around me felt the same way. As the service began we sang some of the songs I remembered from the church in Bowling Green. That helped calm my nerves. As Denny began his sermon an elderly woman I was sitting next to took my hand in hers. At first I didn't know what to do, so I did nothing at all. Every time the preacher would make a point she would give my hand a squeeze. She was unaware of what she was doing. I learned later that she and her husband had raised over forty foster children. Dinah quite simply is a magnet who draws to herself people to love. Whenever she is asked why she adopted so many children she responds, "Who else is going to love them if not me?"

That Sunday morning I became one of her children. She and her husband, Bob, had numbered white children as well among their extended family. With the reach of her hand I was also accepted as well. Though it has been years, I still have not found my way completely into the congregation, though I am always more than welcomed. Some lines take years to cross. I can only tell you that my awkward attempt at racial reconciliation is a response to a fragment-ed part of my life, a piece of a puzzle that may never fully come together. All I know is something in me longs to find a place for it to fit.

There comes a moment in our lives when some of the pieces of the puzzle come together—where all our past experiences, both good and bad, are brought to bear in causing us to become who God intends us to be. The encounter of Cornelius was just such a moment in Peter's life.

Everything that had happened to him up until that time came together in the crucible of that moment, causing him to respond in just the way he did. As a result of his reluctant obedience, he was never the same.

All of us bring out "presets" with us into our walk with Jesus. I believe he intends it to be so. So Paul brought with him bits and pieces of his Pharisaism, his passion, his desire for correct theology integrated into life. Peter too brought his agrarian sim-plicity, his practical approach and, as we shall see in the story of Cornelius, his Jewish concern for ritual purity.

It had all begun with Jesus, of course. He made sure that the disciples would not experience anything on their own that he had not first experienced and prepared them for. Peter remembered clearly when Jesus had declared all foods clean (Mark 7:19). He remembered his confusion at returning to the well only to find Jesus talking with a Samaritan woman (John 4:27). Jesus, the true pioneer of reconciliation, had prepared the way for what was to happen in the expansion of the church beyond its Jewish boundaries.

After the church was scattered, due to the persecution that

erupted after the stoning of Stephen, Philip was the first to preach in Samaria (Acts 8:4-13). When the apostles sent Peter and John to see what was happening there, they laid hands on the new believers, who, though they had been baptized, had not received the Holy Spirit. We can only imagine what was going on in John's heart and mind as he laid his hands on a people he had earlier wanted to call down fire upon (Luke 9:54). As they made their way back to Jerusalem, Peter and John preached in many Samaritan cities. All this provided the groundwork for what was to come. The gospel was about to explode to the far corners of the world, and Peter would be the pivotal person.

The effect of Peter's burgeoning openness is hinted at in the ninth chapter of Acts. If you are not careful you will read right past it. In verse 43 we are told that Peter was staying in Joppa beside the sea, in the house of a man named Simon. This would not be so unusual until we read that Simon was a tanner, that is, his job was skinning animals and preparing the hides. This meant that he was constantly in contact with unclean carcasses and their blood and so was considered perpetually unclean. Peter's choice of accommodations reveals that some of his old concerns about his ritual purity were beginning to shift. It is not hard to imagine him believing that he had reached his limit of compromise by staying at Simon's house. It seems a strange choice for a person who chose to live one door down from the synagogue! I wonder if he might even have congratulated himself just a little bit for his magnanimous gesture. Little did he know just how far his faith would be stretched.

In Caesarea there lived a Roman army officer named Cornelius, who was a captain of the Italian Regiment. He was a devout man who feared the God of Israel, as did his entire household. He gave generously to charity and was a man who regularly prayed to God. One afternoon about three o'clock, he had a vision in which he saw an angel of God coming toward him. "Cornelius!" the angel said.

Cornelius stared at him in terror. "What is it, sir?" he asked the angel.

And the angel replied, "Your prayers and gifts to the poor have not gone unnoticed by God! Now send some men down to Joppa to find a man named Simon Peter. He is staying with Simon, a leatherworker who lives near the shore. Ask him to come and visit you."

As soon as the angel was gone, Cornelius called two of his household servants and a devout soldier, one of his personal attendants. He told them what had happened and sent them off to Joppa.

The next day as Cornelius's messengers were nearing the city, Peter went up to the flat roof to pray. It was about noon, and he was hungry. But while lunch was being prepared, he fell into a trance. He saw the sky open, and something like a large sheet was let down by its four corners. In the sheet were all sorts of animals, reptiles, and birds. Then a voice said to him, "Get up, Peter; kill and eat them."

"Never, Lord," Peter declared. "I have never in all my life eaten anything forbidden by our Jewish laws."

The voice spoke again, "If God says something is acceptable, don't say it isn't." The same vision was repeated three times. Then the sheet was pulled up again to heaven.

Peter was very perplexed. What could the vision mean? Just then the men sent by Cornelius found the house and stood outside at the gate. They asked if this was the place where Simon Peter was staying. Meanwhile, as Peter was puzzling over the vision, the Holy Spirit said to him, "Three men have come looking for you. Go down and go with them without hesitation. All is well, for I have sent them."

So Peter went down and said, "I'm the man you are looking for. Why have you come?"

They said, "We were sent by Cornelius, a Roman officer. He is a devout man who fears the God of Israel and is well respected by all the Jews. A holy angel instructed him to send for you so you can go to his house and give him a message."

So Peter invited the men to be his guests for the night. The next day he went with them, accompanied by some other believers from Joppa.

They arrived in Caesarea the following day. Cornelius was waiting for him and had called together his relatives and close friends to meet Peter. As Peter entered his home, Cornelius fell to the floor before him in worship. But Peter pulled him up and said, "Stand up! I'm a human being like you!" So Cornelius got up, and they talked together and went inside where the others were assembled.

Peter told them, "You know it is against the Jewish laws for me to come into a Gentile home like this. But God has shown me that I should never think of anyone as impure. So I came as soon as I was sent for. Now tell me why you sent for me."

Cornelius replied, "Four days ago I was praying in my house at three o'clock in the afternoon. Suddenly, a man in dazzling clothes was standing in front of me. He told me, 'Cornelius, your prayers have been heard, and your gifts to the poor have been noticed by God! Now send some men to Joppa and summon Simon Peter. He is staying in the home of Simon, a leatherworker who lives near the shore.' So I sent for you at once, and it was good of you to come. Now here we are, waiting before God to hear the message the Lord has given you." (Acts 10:1-33)

It is easy to forget that for almost fifteen years Christianity had existed solely as a sect within Judaism, that for the most part its locus of faith was still the temple in Jerusalem. It is clear that there were still those in leadership in the church who desired that things stay that way. James, the brother of Jesus, is the best example. Jesus had been clear in his ecumenicity, though he reached out first to the lost sheep of the house of Israel. He had twice destroyed the marketplace in the temple in order to restore a quiet place so the Gentile "God-fearers" would have a place to pray. The tension had begun to build with the outreach to the Samaritans. Now, with the Cornelius affair, matters will come to a point of crisis. The simple fact that the story is told twice, almost in its entirety, should tell us something significant is happening.

The incident takes place deep in enemy territory. Caesarea was the Roman capital of Judea. The fact that the object of the story is a high-ranking Roman officer makes matters even worse. He represents all that is loathsome to the Jews. But then again we are told that he was "devout." The technical term "God-fearer" (indicating that he was a Gentile who worshiped the God of Israel but would not submit to circumcision in order to become a full proselyte) is used to describe his intimate relationship to Judaism. He also practices two of the central tenets of Jewish piety: he gives to the poor and observes the regular hours of prayer. All this being true, the fact remains that he is still a hated Roman and an unclean Gentile. Despite his affinity for Judaism, no observant Jew would have shared a meal with him, nor even entered into his house. It is important to note that God sent a vision to both Cornelius and Peter to help prepare them for their life-changing experiences.

At three o'clock, one of the regular times of prayer, Cornelius sees in a vision an angel coming toward him. This terrifies him, though he surely had experienced the horrors of primitive warfare. The angel gives him the details of where Peter can be found and instructs him to send for the well-known disciple of Jesus. Cornelius immediately obeys, sending two of his men, one a devout soldier, the other a servant, to Joppa to retrieve Peter. The trip was thirty-two miles along the coastline road.

The Lord knew that Peter needed to be prepared for this encounter as well. The next day, at noon, Peter goes up on the roof of Simon's house to pray. You can imagine him dealing with the offensive atmosphere, with the stench of the tanning process in his nose, imagining he has been stretched about as far as he can go!

While waiting for the noon meal to be prepared, he falls into a trance, literally an "ecstasy." He sees heaven open and a large sheet or perhaps a sail being lowered down to him. To his amazement and disgust, the sail is filled with unclean animals, with all the things he has spent a lifetime avoiding. (If indeed it was a sail that he saw, we see the imagination of God at work, wrapping up what was unfamiliar in something familiar that Peter had known and used every day.)

Saying "No" to God

The ploy does not work. Peter displays one last time one of the consistent facets of his character. He apparently says "no" three times to God. Certainly he must have taken it all as a test. He will not fail by following the voices' instructions and eating what is unclean. His ritual purity, rooted in his own concept of works-righteousness, is the last vestige of his old orthodoxy that needs to go. All at once it is over. The sail is gone. Peter is left alone, puzzled by what it all might mean.

At that precise moment Cornelius's servants arrive. Luke is careful to tell us that they stood outside at the gate and called in for Peter. As Gentiles they are aware that it is not allowed for them to enter and defile a Jewish home, even one that smells like Simon's!

Peter goes down to meet them and hears for the first time a story he will retell for the rest of his life. Since it is evening, he makes the remarkable gesture of inviting them into the house to stay the night. The only thing worse than a tanner's house is a tanner's house full of Gentiles!

When they arrive at Cornelius's house the next day, they find that a hungry crowd has already gathered there to hear what Peter has to say. The level of Cornelius's expectation is revealed when he falls down before Peter as if to worship him. After all, he was just yesterday talking to an angel about Peter. Peter, horrified at the prospect, tells him to get up. He is only an ordinary man like Cornelius.

As they are making their way together into the house, Peter says at first what any good Jewish man should say at the prospect of entering a Gentile home: "You know I'm not supposed to be here." But somewhere along the way, perhaps as he walked beside the sea, as he had done so many times with Jesus, Peter had put two and two together. The central category of his life, his concepts of "clean and unclean," had come into direct conflict with the light of his ecstasy. Though the dream had been about food, Peter understood that he had wrongly extended the notion of clean and unclean to people. The vision had exposed the hypocrisy in his heart and in the heart of his beliefs. He had avoided "unclean" people like the forbidden foods he had been raised to loathe. Yet God had created people, all people. Jesus, Peter knew, had died so that the distinction between clean and unclean could be subjugated. Jesus could make anyone clean—even the last person on earth he might expect to be clean: a Roman soldier, one of the very ones who had crucified Jesus!

What an earthquake this caused in Peter's soul! It was a direct assault on one of his most basic beliefs. But Jesus had come to shatter and redefine everything. Certainly it is a shattered Simon who makes his way, for the first time in his life, into the Gentile dwelling. He will find there men and women, like himself, who want nothing less than to eat the true bread of heaven. People who, though they live in darkness, have nonetheless seen a great Light!

A Gentile Pentecost

As Peter makes his way into the house, he finds there every preacher's dream: a large, hungry congregation. With tears in his eyes, he shares with them his new realization. "Now I see that it is true," he whispers, "God does not show favoritism!" His image of God, so challenged and stretched by his time with Jesus, has grown now even more. The crowd he would have earlier crossed the street to avoid, would have denied meal fellowship with, seems now bathed in a new light. He sees bright eyes and hungry faces. He looks out at men and women, boys and girls who will suffer every bit as much as he will in the years to come for their allegiance to Jesus. He looks out on brothers and sisters.

As we saw earlier, he will not even make it through his sermon before the Holy Spirit, who so longs to embrace all men and women, will interrupt him and pour himself out on them all. Peter does not even have a chance to lay hands on them, as he had done for the Samaritan believers. This is completely a work of God, Peter realizes. It is a lesson he will carry with him all his life.

From this point on, true leadership in the church will be exercised only by those who are willing to listen to the Spirit. Only those who are able to embrace and preserve the universal vision that Peter glimpsed there in the house of Cornelius will be fit shepherds. The task will never again be a matter of guarding the old orthodoxy. From this day on it will be new wine in new wineskins.

Peter will pay a price he seems completely willing to sacrifice for this new radical obedience. He will be confronted by the leadership of the Jerusalem church and criticized for eating with Gentiles (Acts 11). He will not take the high moral ground, but will humbly try to explain to them what it is God is doing in the church and in the world. He will tell them the story, word for word, once again. He will try to appease them by quoting Gamaliel: "Who was I to think I could oppose God?" Though they are said to have no further objection, though it is said they even praise God that the Gentiles had received life, the issue will surface again at the council of Jerusalem, where Peter and Paul will together try to articulate for them the mystery of what God is doing. The council will nod in agreement but still issue a decree advising the Gentiles to maintain a semblance of Jewishness. Peter and Paul will be given the assignment to distribute the decision to the churches, which they will humbly fulfill (though, when faced with the same questions again and again, neither of them will ever—not one time—refer to the words of the council's decree).

Peter, the unquestioned leader of the church until this time, will now virtually disappear onto the mission field. James will become the leader of the Jerusalem church, a congregation whose influence will wane in the years to follow. Later it will be the Gentiles who will contribute to the relief fund for the Jerusalem saints. And Paul, without an ounce of bitterness, will zealously collect that fund for them.

The same pattern we saw so clearly in the life of Jesus we see now in Peter's life. When Jesus worked a miracle, all the Pharisees would see was an infraction of their rules. For Peter, it is Jewish Christians (oddly enough) who struggle to see the miracle of God's reaching out to the whole world through the infraction of a rule. Like the Pharisees, many of whom were now leaders in the church, the Jewish Christians still see clean and unclean as categories to apply to people as well as food.

Peter disappears into a sea of these so-called unclean. His missionary pastorate is based first in Antioch, where they were first derisively called "Christians." This would be the first place where the Christians would stand out distinctively from the Jewish community. Next many believe he went to Corinth, and finally to Rome.

The person Peter eventually becomes is a direct consequence of his experience with Cornelius. In his final words in Acts, you can hear the pathos in his voice:

> Brothers, you know that some time ago God made a choice among you that the Gentiles might hear from my lips the message of the gospel and believe. God, who knows the heart, showed that he accepted them by giving the Holy Spirit to them, just as he did to us. He made no distinction between us and them, for he purified their hearts by faith. Now then, why do you try to test God by putting on the necks of the disciples a yoke that neither we nor our fathers have been able to bear? No! We believe it is through the grace of our Lord Jesus that we are saved, just as they are. (Acts 15:7-11 NIV)

Even as Jesus chose to let go of power and authority, so Peter lets go as well. He never forgot the lesson in the upper room, that true greatness involves taking up the basin and the towel. He would wash feet with the water of Jesus' word for the remainder of his life.

There are a thousand ways to wash feet. It might take the form of a cup of cold water offered in Jesus' name. Perhaps it might be a simple touch on the shoulder. For Peter it was the willingness to go someplace he knew he was not supposed to be in obedience to Jesus' call, to cross a line no one had ever crossed before. For Dinah in that Tennessee church, it was holding the hand of a nervous white man who didn't even know why he had sat down in her world. If she didn't love me, who else would?

CHAPTER EIGHTEEN

The Passionate Writer

1-2 PETER

I noted previously how Jesus and Peter tended to define each other during their early years of ministry together. This was most clearly seen in the Caesarea Philippi confession.

"Who am I?" Jesus asks in essence.

"You are the Christ," Peter responds.

"You are the Rock," Jesus completes the exchange.

True friends define each other. Over their two and a half to three years together they became the truest of friends. Jesus even says as much to Peter and the others (John 15:14-15).

Writing his letters sometime before A.D. 65, Peter extends the defining quality of that precious relationship to you and me! (See 1 Peter 2:11; 4:12; 2 Peter 1:10; 3:1, 8, 14, 17.) In the course of that passionate correspondence he defines us. He tells us who we are: We are pilgrims and strangers (1 Peter 1:1; 2:11). We are newborn babies (2:2) and obedient children (1:14). We are free slaves of God (2:16), an elect race, a royal priesthood, a holy nation, God's own possession (2:9). We are the flock of God (5:2). In these days, when the church is seeking so desperately for an understanding of what it is, the letters of Peter must become a central focus for us. And yet they are so rarely preached on or even referred to. The focus of most Christian scholarship in the last several years has tragically been merely to discount the authorship of Peter's second letter.

The two letters were written to a mixed group of Gentile and Jewish Christians, an appropriate flock for a shepherd who had sacrificed so much to bring the two together. They lived in and around Asia Minor in the areas of Pontus, Galatia, Cappadocia, Asia and Bithynia. This is the area Paul was forbidden to enter in Acts 16:7 (see also Romans 15:20). The listing of these areas is the only hint we have of the focus of Peter's missionary activity in the later years of his life. There is no other evidence of his ministering in these locations besides this list.

Some scholars note an absence of the kind of personal greetings Paul's letters demonstrate. They conclude from this that Peter actually never visited these areas in person, since it appears he knows no one personally there. This argument is hardly conclusive.

The letters are a remarkable mirror to the sermons of Peter in Acts. Like his sermons, they are filled with Old Testament references. Although he has paid an enormous price to step beyond the thoroughly Jewish world he grew up in, he still thinks like a Jewish man of his time. He must substantiate from the Old Testament everything he understands and feels. He particularly loves the story of Noah, it seems. It is the only story referred to in both letters (1 Peter 3:20; 2 Peter 2:5)—understandable for a man who grew up in a boat!

The letters display Peter's unique and often graphic vocabulary. Again and again he stresses the passionate need to "love one another deeply" (1 Peter 1:22; 3:8; 4:8 NIV). His language becomes particularly harsh in 2 Peter 2:10-22 when he describes "proud and arrogant" men who are causing harm to the church. Age and years of hardship on the mission trail have not dimmed the passionate intensity of the man we first came to know in the Gospels.

Also, as with the sermons in Acts, much of Peter's vocabulary is unique, often made up. One hundred nineteen words in his letters appear nowhere else in the New Testament. He alludes to the writings of his friend and companion Paul eighteen times; most of these references, fifteen of them, come from Romans, and most of these come from the thirteenth chapter. Perhaps, as for so many of us, it was his favorite book!

Peter's experience with Jesus is woven into the narratives (1 Peter 2:21-24; 5:1-10). So many of the themes that dominated their lives come out in the letters. The concept of innocent suffering becomes absolutely central to Peter's understanding of what faith in Jesus means. Peter reflects Jesus' strong emphasis on prayer as well—that the Christian life must be shaped by prayer (1 Peter 3:7; 4:7).

The only historical incident to which Peter makes reference is his experience with Jesus at the transfiguration. In his second letter Peter reminds his readers that he was an eyewitness to the majesty of Jesus (1:16-18), that he himself heard the "majestic splendor" saying, "This is my beloved Son; I am fully pleased with him."

Now, as the church experiences persecution, they need an eyewitness like Peter to remind them that the Lord they serve, whom they hope will soon return in glory, at one time revealed that splendor.

Of particular interest is a shift that occurs in his first letter. In the first half Peter refers to suffering as a somewhat distant prospect. The focus of the early part of the letter is preparation for a future experience of suffering. In 4:12, however, a distinct shift seems to have occurred.

"Don't be surprised at the fiery trials you are going through," he writes. It would seem that a fresh crisis is upon the church. It seems clear that this statement represents the persecution that was breaking out all over the empire as a result of the great fire in Rome. The Roman historian Tacitus tells us that after the great fire in the summer of A.D. 64, Nero used the Christians as scapegoats:

> Nero fabricated scapegoats and punished with every refinement the notoriously depraved Christians (as they were first popularly called). . . . First, Nero had self-acknowledged Christians arrested. Then, on their information, large numbers of others were condemned—not so much for incendiarism as for their anti-social tendencies. Their deaths were made farcical. Dressed in the skins of wild animals, they were torn to pieces by dogs, or crucified, or made into torches to be ignited after dark as substitutes for daylight. (*Annals* XV.44)

This ancient account allows us to understand the dangerous situation the Christians to whom Peter was writing were facing. Earlier in the letter he had assured them by saying, "Now, who will want to harm you if you are eager to do good?" (3:13). But now the situation has radically changed, and Peter understands that they will be indiscriminately persecuted. Until we understand this life situation, we will never appreciate the passionate purpose of the letters.

Finally, Peter's letters represent a poignant farewell. Jesus had earlier told him about the manner of his death, had strongly hinted that it would entail crucifixion (John 21:18). Now he has been given to understand that his own "exodus" is near (2 Peter 1:13-15). So, remarkably, we have in the letters, especially the second letter, his last will and testament. He is clearly burdened by the threat of false teachers who have infiltrated the churches. He will encapsulate his last spiritual advice in two passages. In the first, 1 Peter 3:8-9, he condenses his admonition to five simple imperatives: live in harmony, be sympathetic, love deeply, be compassionate and humble, and bless those who do you evil. His advice might also be seen as a sketch of his spiritual life, of all that Jesus has accomplished in his own spirit over the years. The admonitions are a pencil portrait of his emotional life.

The second and final capsule comes in the opening of the final letter (1:5-8). This statement has been rightly called the "Ladder of Faith," for each concept builds on the former (Paul delighted in the same type of "chain sayings": Romans 5:3-5; Galatians 4:4-7; 1 Timothy 6:11-12).

> So make every effort to apply the benefits of these promises to your life. Then your faith will produce a life of moral excellence. A life of moral excellence leads to knowing God better. Knowing God leads to self-control. Self-control leads to patient endurance, and patient endurance leads to godliness. Godliness leads to love for other Christians, and finally, you will grow to

have genuine love for everyone. (2 Peter 1:5-7)

The bookends of this remarkable statement (a statement that requires a lifetime to meditate on and understand): *faith* and *love*. These might be said to be the bookends of Peter's own spiritual journey. What began with a remarkable statement of faith at Caesarea Philippi ended in a missionary life defined and dominated by love. This amazing pillar, perhaps the last living link to Jesus besides John, the one called the Rock, simply and humbly identifies himself as the "fellow elder" (1 Peter 5:1). He has poured out his life trying to obey Jesus' final admonition to feed and care for his sheep. He has lost everything for the sake of the call—his possessions, his authority. As he looks his own death squarely in the face, he fearlessly thinks only of the fate of the little flock he will leave behind. And he writes for them and for us these two precious letters.

Epilogue

THE FAITHFUL MARTYR

The sources are fragmentary and often conflicting in regard to the last years of Peter's life. As best we can reconstruct them, his last fifteen years were spent on the mission field, as a missionary pastor visiting and encouraging young churches. Paul mentions the fact that his wife often accompanied him (1 Corinthians 9:5).

Exactly when he traveled to Rome for the last time is hotly debated. It is widely believed that Peter came in response to a request from Paul to help with a problem in the church at Rome. While Peter was there, he was caught up in the persecution of the church by Nero, around the time of the great fire in July of 64 (Lactantius *Deaths of the Persecutors* 2, 5). The sources agree that Paul and Peter died at the same time (Eusebius *HE* 2.25.5).

Paul was beheaded, as befitted a Roman citizen. Peter was crucified upside down in the Circus of Nero, "near the obelisk between the goals," where the Vatican now stands (Eusebius *HE* 3.1.2-3). He was buried close by on Vatican hill. Recent excavations beneath the Vatican have probably unearthed his grave. Paul was buried along the Appian Way. His grave is now lost.

And so the fragile stone was finally broken, crucified upside down, a victim, says Clement, of the unwarranted jealousy of Nero

(Origen *HE* 3.1.2-3). The Roman historian Seneca recorded seeing men crucified in all different positions, including upside down. It is said Peter requested this peculiar form of crucifixion because he considered himself unworthy to die in the same way Jesus had.

From simple fisherman to struggling disciple to first confessor, from despairing denier to fearless leader, from ambitious go-getter to humble servant. The progression (though infinitely more complicated) goes something like that. It is indeed miraculous that Jesus chose someone like Peter, a man we all identify with in one way or another, a person who teaches us more through his weaknesses than his strengths.

He humbly turns the title "Rock," which eventually became his true name, into an invitation, for in his eyes we are all supposed to be "living stones." But without a doubt, he was the first of these stones to be laid, the foundational disciple. The pride that led him at first to join in the debates about who was the greatest was definitively defeated in the course of his walk with Jesus.

Eugene Peterson, in his introduction to Peter's letters, says it wonderfully:

> The way Peter handled himself in that position of power is even more impressive than the power itself. He stayed out of the center, didn't "wield" power, maintained a scrupulous subordination to Jesus. Given his charismatic personality and well-deserved position at the head, he could easily have taken over, using the prominence of his association with Jesus to promote himself. That he didn't do it, given the frequency with which spiritual leaders do exactly that, is impressive.

Peter is a breath of fresh air.

(from the introduction to 1 Peter in The Message)

Peter kept finding himself caught in the middle. He would come into conflict with Paul, fifteen years after the Cornelius affair, over the same question of reconciliation. Paul's greatest strength was also his greatest weakness. He had brought into the new faith his pharisaic "presets." Among those the most prominent was the desire to "get it right." You might call it theological exactitude. Peter's presets were totally different. They were more agrarian. He brought with him the concern to be in the right place, to use the right bait, whether to catch fish or men. He was more patient, it seems to me. Though Paul had known brokenness, it was not to the degree Peter had known it.

Peter would find himself finally in a completely unfamiliar and pagan environment in Rome. But the call of Jesus had placed him there, and he would obey even if it meant death on a cross. They would die together, Peter and Paul, the pillars.

An Invitation

I'll leave you where we first met, at that ancient monastery in the hills of Romania. Take a step back with me and let's look at the entire picture, painted there on the wall. There they both are, Peter and Paul. And between them they are holding up the church, Christ's church. The ancient painter, in his quiet simplicity, understood then what we have forgotten: we desperately need them both. We need the passion for correctness that we find in Paul. But we also need the stable bridge of Peter to continue to help us cross over. We need his courage and his simplicity. Above all, we need to gain from him the power to let go—to let go of possessions and power, to let go of position and authority, to give in at last, as he finally did, to the service of the basin and the towel with all its bitter consequences.

If we are to be "living stones," if the church is to go on being built the way Jesus desires it to be built, then Peter's story must in some sense become our story. Only then will our story become like Peter's, the story of Jesus.

In closing then, hear again Peter's gracious invitation to join him in becoming living stones: Come to Christ, who is the living cornerstone of God's temple. He was rejected by the people, but he is precious to God who chose him.

And now God is building you, as living stones, into his spiritual temple.

BIBLIOGRAPHY

BOOKS ON PETER

Allies, T. W. *St. Peter: His Name and His Office*. London: Catholic Truth Society, 1895.

Brown, Raymond E., Karl P. Donfried and John Reumann, eds. *Peter in the New Testament*. New York: Paulist, 1983.

Butler, John B. *Peter: The Illustrious Disciple*. Clinton, Ia.: LBC, 1993.

Cullmann, Oscar. *Peter: Disciple-Apostle-Martyr*. Translated by Floyd Filoson. 1953; reprint, London: SCM Press, 1962.

Elton, Godfrey. *Simon Peter: A Study of Discipleship*. London: Peter Davis, 1965.

Fickett, Harold L. *Profiles in Clay*. Los Angeles: Cowman, 1963.

Gill, David W. *Peter the Rock*. Downers Grove, Ill.: InterVarsity Press, 1986.

Grant, Michael. *Saint Peter: A Biography*. New York: Scribner, 1994.

Huntsperger, Larry. *The Fisherman: A Novel*. Grand Rapids, Mich.: Revell, 2003.

Martin, Hugh. *Simon Peter*. 1869; reprint, Edinburgh: Banner of Truth, 1967.

Meyer, F. B. *The Life of Peter*. Lynwood, Wash.: Emerald, 1996.

Patten, John. *Simon Peter's Ordination Day*. London: James Clarke, 1935.

Perkins, Pheme. *Peter: Apostle for the Whole Church*. Minneapolis: Fortress, 2000.

Thiede, Carsten P. *Simon Peter: From Galilee to Rome*. Grand Rapids, Mich.: Academie, 1986.

Underhill, Francis. *Saint Peter*. London: Centenary, 1937.

HISTORICAL BACKGROUND STUDIES

Akenson, Donald Harman. *Saint Paul: A Skeleton Key to the Historical Jesus*. London: Oxford University Press, 2000.

Arrington, French L. *The Acts of the Apostles: An Introduction and Commentary*. Peabody, Mass.: Hendrickson, 1988.

Bacon, David Francis. *Lives of the Apostles*. New Haven, Conn.: Hitchcock and Stafford, 1835.

Barrett, C. K. *The New Testament Background: Selected Documents*. San Francisco: Harper & Row, 1987.

Bonhoeffer, Dietrich. *The Cost of Discipleship*. Translated by R. H. Fuller. London: SCM Press, 1948.

Bray, Gerald, ed. *James, 1-2 Peter, 1-3 John, Jude*. Ancient Christian Commentary on Scripture. Downers Grove, Ill.: InterVarsity Press, 2000.

Brown, Raymond E. *An Introduction to the New Testament*. New York: Doubleday, 1996.

Bruce, F. F. *The Book of the Acts*. New International Commentary on the New Testament. Grand Rapids, Mich.: Eerdmans, 1988.

Ferguson, Everett. *Early Christians Speak*. Abilene, Kans.: ACU Press, 1987.

Grant, Michael. *The Jews in the Roman World*. New York: Barnes & Noble Books, 1973.

Jeffers, James S. *The Greco-Roman World of the New Testament Era*. Downers Grove, Ill.: InterVarsity Press, 1999.

Jeremias, Joachim. *Jerusalem in the Time of Jesus*. Philadelphia: Fortress, 1969.

Jurgens, William A. *The Faith of the Early Fathers, Volume 1*. Collegeville, Minn.: Liturgical Press, 1970.

Lane, William L. Mark. *The Gospel According to Mark*. Grand Rapids, Mich.: Eerdmans, 1974.

Leon-Dufour, Xavier. *Dictionary of the New Testament*. San Francisco: Harper & Row, 1983.

Lohse, Eduard. *The New Testament Environment*. Nashville: Abingdon, 1976.

Eusebius. *Eusebius—The Church History: A New Translation with Commentary*. Translation and commentary by Paul L. Maier. Grand Rapids, Mich.: Kregel, 1999.

McVey, Kathleen E. *Ephrem the Syrian: Hymns*. New York: Paulist, 1989.

Meeks, Wayne A. *The First Urban Christians: The Social World of the Apostle Paul*. London: Yale University Press, 1983.

Painter, John. *Just James: The Brother of Jesus in History and Tradition*. Columbia: University of South Carolina Press, 1997.

Stambaugh, John E., and David L. Balch. *The New Testament in Its Social Environment*. Philadelphia: Westminster Press, 1986.

Stott, John R. W. *The Story of the New Testament*. Grand Rapids, Mich.: Baker, 1994.

About the Author

MICHAEL CARD is an award-winning musician, performing artist and the writer of many popular songs, including the classics "El Shaddai" and "Immanuel." He has produced over twenty albums, including *Scribbling in the Sand: The Best of Michael Card Live* and his latest release, *A Fragile Stone*. He is also the author of numerous books, including *Scribbling in the Sand* and *The Parable of Joy*.

Card has been a mentor to many younger artists and musicians, teaching courses on the creative process and calling the Christian recording industry to deeper discipleship. He lives in Tennessee with his wife and four children.

Card holds an undergraduate degree in biblical studies from Western Kentucky University in 1979. He also had an assistantship and taught physics and astronomy in a masters program at WKU. Michael went on to receive a master's degree in biblical studies from Western Kentucky University in 1980. He is currently working on his doctorate in classical literature.

In cooperation with The Bible League, Michael Card has launched the Michael Card Share the Word Project to provide Bibles to persecuted Christians and searching people. For over ten years Card has partnered with The Bible League's efforts to supply Bibles to people around the world. For more information, contact The Michael Card Share the Word Project, c/o Bible League, P.O. Box 28000, Chicago, IL 60628, or e-mail info@bibleleague.org or visit <www.mcsharetheword.org>.

For more information about
the ministry and music of Michael Card, contact:

The Card Group, LLC
(615) 790-7675
E-mail: info@michaelcard.com
Or go to: www.michaelcard.com